A SKINFUL OF SCOTCH

A SKINFUL

with drawings by
HARTLEY RAMSAY

CLIFFORD HANLEY

OF SCOTCH

HOUGHTON MIFFLIN COMPANY BOSTON
THE RIVERSIDE PRESS CAMBRIDGE
1965

ALSO BY CLIFFORD HANLEY

Second Time Round

SECOND PRINTING R

Copyright © 1965 by Clifford Hanley
All rights reserved including the right to
reproduce this book or parts thereof in any form
Library of Congress Catalog Card Number: 65-19313

Chapter 3, "Check That Pladdie, Laddie," first
appeared in the summer 1965 issue of *Horizon*
under the title "Kilt Complex."

Printed in the United States of America

This book is for
Iain and Jean

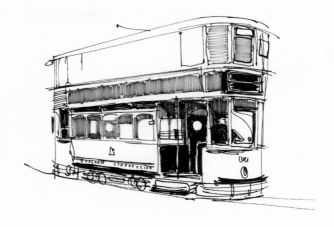

CONTENTS

INTRODUCTION

On reading through this book, I discover one notorious Scottish, or Scotch, topic cropping up so often that I fear I may have written a Boozer's Guide to Bonnie Scotland. This wasn't the idea at all; it's simply that so many things that come back to mind are crystal clear because they were fuzzy at the time, or they might never have happened. The monotonous unintentional insistence on drink is balanced by the relative absence of sex, which fact should please the most exacting observer because nobody minds being affronted by drink, but people go livid if you blab about sex. As the Kirk elder from Ross-shire reported after visiting London, sex is only in its infancy in this parish, and we plan to keep it that way.

The book is a rag-bag, and the chapter headings are no guarantee of anything since each chapter tried to begin with something but usually became distracted on the way. Where it appears unpatriotic or treasonable, the explanation is that Scotsmen, even mushy sentimentalists like myself, are so carried away by the sheer allure of the place that they have to curl their lips or they would give themselves away. We have to preserve the image of the dour, belittling Scot simply because we know that the Scot is an extravagant, histrionic romantic who requires disguise so that foreigners will keep buying his woollens and ships and beef bulls under the delusion that they came from a hard-headed country where business is business.

Scotland is a small country consisting of Highland mountains, lowland valleys and southern hills, together with a mess of islands to the north and west. It has a population of five million. The majority nominal religion is Presbyterian Christianity, sub-divided into

various churches of which the largest is the Church of Scotland; but there is a sizeable Roman Catholic minority and a vigorous Jewish community and away out in the Atlantic you can find a good-going mosque on the island of Lewis. There are noticeable and long-established strains from Italy and Poland and a growing population of Pakistanis. The game of golf was invented at St Andrews, as if that mattered.

The country enjoys uneventful relations with its larger neighbour England, most of the time. The two kingdoms were united under one crown in 1603 when James VI of Scotland became James I. The Scottish Parliament was absorbed into the English Parliament in 1707. The culture and the history of the two countries had never been entirely parallel, however, and have never *entirely* converged. After conquering England, the Romans intended to mop up Scotland, but became either frightened or bored and abandoned the idea. The weather can be miserable at times. But the rigours of the climate are much exaggerated, mostly by Scotsmen, from a twisted sense of pride. Sunshine in Scotland is glorious, and there are regular droughts in the Western Isles during summers which drown the South of England.

The name Scotland is an importation from Ireland, brought by a migrant tribe. The principal racial strains of the people were Celtic,

from the mysterious people who came through Iberia on their way to somewhere, and Nordic from the Scandinavians who turned up regularly for trade, or a fight, or a change from those soap-faced blonde Northern women. The Norwegian composer Grieg was the grandson of an Aberdeenshire farmer, Greig, who may well have been descended from another Norwegian himself. Until the Norwegians built their railway in 1905, in fact, it was easier and faster to travel from Bergen to Aberdeen than from Bergen to the capital Oslo.

The colloquial dialects spoken in Scotland are independent productions, and in no way corruptions of a 'standard' English English. They developed from different sources, mainly Teutonic. Many Norse words and phrases, as for example stoorsooker (vacuum-cleaner), are identical in sound to broad Scots-English. Living close to the sea, the Scots have always been travellers, though never ever colonisers in the imperial sense. Before the country was united with England, the natives tended to have more commerce with France than with their immediate neighbour. Claret and brandy were favourite Scottish tipples before Scotch whisky became respectable, which happened barely a century ago. Many words of French origin have passed into common use in Scots-English, and it is even possible that the Scotch feast of Hogmanay is a form of Au gui Menez (Lead on to the mistletoe).

Dunmore, Beauly

Every Scotsman regards himself as an authority on the works of Robert Burns, even if he is not; on boats of every kind, even if he is not; on whisky, even if he is not; and on the brotherhood of man, since one of the five lines of Burns he actually remembers is Man to Man the world o'er shall brithers be for a' that. The country helped to cradle the first Industrial Revolution, which left parts of it in an awful mess, and consequently the working-class movement, which gave rise to the famous Red Clydeside. Heavy dependence on old heavy industries has made it vulnerable to depressions and unemployment. The Highlands and islands have always been in a state of progressive depopulation. There are as many Scots, or Scots descendants, all over the world as there are in Scotland itself. As soon as they settle in another country, Scotsmen inaugurate a St Andrews Society, and Englishmen join it.

The Scot, like the Negro and the Jew, has the conviction that his people have been exploited and betrayed, and although he has not suffered as these groups have and has no restrictions on him as an individual, he tends to be aggressively Scottish at small provocation. At the same time, having been born outside the English class system, he lives above it, and has no hesitation in exploiting the English if he

migrates across the Border. Wyatt Earp, the Dodge City marshal who cleaned up the west by bending his gun-barrel round the skulls of innocent drunks, is believed to have been partly Scottish by descent.

Scotsmen, however, vary as much as any other people. There are Scottish heroes and Scottish cowards, geniuses and idiots, savages and saints. If there is an average, he is mildly bellicose in his talk and kindly disposed to people, and crazily extravagant with his money.

The land, outside the Lowland corners where the rotten tooth-stumps of nineteenth century industry are still standing, is awesome in beauty. There are rolling farmlands prodigious in yield and efficiency, glens heavy with fruit, singing rivers and seascapes of terrifying masculinity; and the colours of mountains and islands and lochs are disbelieved when recorded on colour film. It is never a bore.

The songs of the country are stirring or tender or unbearably sad. The genuine patriotic songs like 'Scots Wha Hae' are concerned with defying the world, however big, and damning death for a trifle. There are hundreds of songs wrapped up in exile and death, including the most famous Scottish song of all. 'Ye'll tak' the high road and

I'll tak' the low road, and I'll be in Scotland afore ye; but me and my true love will never meet again on the bonnie bonnie banks o' Loch Lomond.' The lyric is put in the mouth of a lassie whose young lover was to be executed in London for rebellion, and the high road is the road to heaven, and not Loch Lomond. The song of exile is almost as large a form as the blues of the American Negro, and for the same reasons. From the lone shieling and the misty island, mountains divide us and a waste of seas; the exile sings. Or, 'Oh for one sight of my bonnie Loch Leven – oh for one hour on the heathery brae, oh for to hear the sweet voice of my dearie calling her cows at the close of the day.'

The hymn to Annie Laurie, modestly written by Lady Nairn, has imposed itself on every English-speaking romantic. And every man's love is like a red, red rose. The nation that worships Robert Burns and recklessly blusters that he is a better man than Shakespeare or Goethe is whistling in the dark of its own stubborn chauvinism, and seizing the excuse for a licensed evening of drink, but it is also responding to the sad sweet spirit that sang, 'Wi' lichtsome heart I pu'd a rose, fu' sweet upon its thorny tree. And my fause lover stole my rose, but ah! he left the thorn wi' me.'

The Scots are great engineers and dancers, strait-laced and libidinously romantic. They're maddening.

STERN AND WILD

The real Scotsman of song and story is a gigantic chiel, swinging a kilt and sporting a mop of flaming red hair and swinging a claymore, and you don't get many of them. There are more Highlanders in the city of Glasgow than there are in the Highlands, and anyway, there are the two strains at least of Highlander, one big and blond or red-haired and the other black in the hair and sallow in the face, like Spaniards or the wee black men of Ireland. Alastair MacTavish Dunnett, the editor of *The Scotsman*, looks more like a Spanish grandee than a bluff Northerner, and maybe he is, if you could look back far enough.

The vanishing Highlander was helped to vanish by a fiscal exercise known as the Highland Clearances, during which the hereditary chieftains of the old Highland clans discovered that they looked like landowners to the English Government, and that they could turn their old paternal responsibilities into money by heaving the clansmen out, or burning them out where necessary, and putting in sheep instead, or deer. Lowland Scots feel a patriotic bitterness about the Clearances to this day, because an old bitterness is a comfortable thing to own, but their admiration for the modern Highlander is well mixed with suspicion because he is still liable to speak Gaelic and be saying God knows what behind your back, and as far as an outsider can tell, he seems to be doing all right despite the terrible tale of woe. Sometimes there's something in it. I have a teuchter[1] friend, Bill Macaskill, from some ludicrously faraway spot like Lochinver, who had worked for so long in Glasgow that people mistook him at sight

[1] teuchter: a derisive Lowland name for a Highlander.

Kyleakin, Skye

for an ordinary person, and he was taking his motorbike to the Hebrides one year and arrived at Kyle of Lochalsh to discover that nobody would let him on board the boat for another three hours. Wet and impatient, he forgot his thin veneer of civilisation and with it the English language and loosed an obscenity of Gaelic at the crew, at which they immediately smiled and replied with cheery greetings in the old tongue and helped him on board without another objection.

My own difficulty, the first time I met the Highlands, was to get anybody to speak Gaelic at all; not that I would have understood it, but I enjoyed the music of the language, which as every Scotsman knows was the tongue they spoke in the Garden of Eden. This happened on a grim cold night of snowstorms one January (my meeting with the Highlands, I mean, not the blethers in Eden) when I travelled into the magic territory in a McBrayne's bus, with driven snow swirling across the windscreen and the cold of the Arctic in the shoes. I kept warm by sharing a fake tartan travelling rug with a girl called Anna, whom I had married a few hours previously, and we were heading for Tarbert, Loch Fyne – not too far into the Highlands, but far enough in a blizzard, and an odd place to be going at all outside the four days of summer. But the bus runs, come blizzard or monsoon. West Highlanders Unite, they always say, You Have Nothing to Lose but McBraynes.

When we were ushered out in the shrieking darkness of Tarbert, we scampered through the weather to the Castle Hotel and fell into a warm welcome and a big hot dinner whose details escape me, but

the important thing is that very soon it was clear that wild celebrations were afoot somewhere through the walls. It turned out that
since it was Saturday, the Tarbert fishermen were home and sharing
out the week's takings, and they do this in the bars of the village, and
sing if they feel like it, and with noseyness unbecoming to a bridal
couple (we were an eccentric bridal couple or we wouldn't have been
there at all) we went down to the lounge to savour the local atmosphere.

What really bothered us was that a gallant fisher laddie was
battering at the piano and singing, not the Dunvegan Song or the
Mull Fisherman's Gaelic howl, but 'Oh Johnnie,' which made a
come-back in the charts that year. It sounded bizarre in a Highland
lilt, too. In a few minutes two burly nautical character-actors edged
in beside us, and the bigger one, who was quite big, with a huge face
dusted with white stubble like a frozen turnip, smiled winningly and
said,

'You'll be on your honeymoon, I suppose.'

This sounded like superb deduction, considering that nobody
except a honeymooner or a Russian spy would have been anywhere
near Tarbert in that weather, so we admitted it. I looked truculent,
in case any jokes were coming. What you must understand is that
there is no way of phoneticising the way a Highlander speaks. You
can double all the S's, because in some areas the lilt is heavily sibi-
lant, but there is no way of indicating how the vowels lengthen, and
the O sounds acquire an aspirate undertone, and the English language is transformed into a slow swooping dance instead of a mere
method of communication. English spoken by a Gaelic-bred West
Highlander is a seductive song.

The other fisherman nodded happily, with the beginnings of a
glaze over his light blue eyes. He was a wee man, hardly as big as
myself but nearly spherical in build.

'Yes,' big John was saying, 'Yes, we was saying as much, Angus
and me here, we was saying as much when we saw you getting off
the bus as we was standing in the doorway of the other hotel, Angus
was saying to me, "now there is a fine big wumman for you, you
don't see many like that nowadays," he was saying, and I was just
saying to Angus here, "no, you don't," I was saying, and I was saying, "and I bet you that wee bugger's her man".'

This is what you call the natural diplomacy of the Highland
gentleman, and at the worst, a Highlander can get away with murder

because if he means any harm, it's a simple kind of harm and he is hardly aware of it himself. It was a wild night in Tarbert that night anyway, and the minute we asked for Gaelic songs we got more than I will ever remember, while I could imagine the Argyllshire police patrolling nearby – determined to enforce the law but unwilling to embarrass anybody by overdoing it.

Something strange and remote always happened to me in the Highlands and the Hebrides, beginning with the day when I sailed past the abandoned isle of St Kilda in a cruise boat and cringed at the sheer brutal height of the cliffs and tried to feel poetic while I was being more seasick than ever before or since. St Kilda wasn't emptied out by the Clearances. It was too far away for any landlord to worry about. It died of its own accord when the young people left for the mainland and life became impossible for the old ones and the children left behind.

Lewis and Harris are one island, the northern hump of the long string of the Outer Hebrides, and this is a trip I made by McBraynes again, by the McBrayne cargo boat *Lochdunvegan* this time, which makes a weekly trip with the bicycle spares and wrapped bread and packets of detergent. I was travelling as a half-passenger, half-crew thing, and lived like a king and was allowed to operate the cargo-loading derrick, a beautiful piece of electrical design from Sweden and exactly what any man would like for Christmas. I omitted to switch it off properly and half-an-hour later the first officer had to dive off the bridge to prevent the hook from being hauled bodily through the sheave. They loved me on that trip to Stornoway.

Stornoway is a shock for the city slicker who pictures the Hebrides as low black houses and heather hills, because it is down-right metropolitan, with street lights and a Woolworth's and every-thing. It is the Hebrides nevertheless, and the Highland Character distilled. It was here that Lord Leverhulme poured out his millions and his dreams to manufacture prosperity for the islanders and found that they didn't want to be bothered, though forty years later the crofters have formed a co-operative for scientific farming and the island is humming with hope. It isn't so long since the curse of the island – and other islands in the group – was the dread tuberculosis, which the islanders accepted with shame and fatalism. TB is usually imagined to be a disease of the congested city, but it raged in the Hebrides among families who lived overcrowded lives in the smoky little cottages in spite of all the raw fresh air blowing over the land,

Near Broadford, Skye

and they were the despair of the medical authorities. When a Lewis-man was told he was tubercular, no matter how slightly, his response was to take to bed and turn his face to the wall to die.

Insanity was another environmental hazard. A terrible lot of nonsense has been talked about this, and wild stories about the in-breeding in the islands that produced every kind of monstrosity, but there was always some small basis of fact in the myths. A girl with relatives in the moribund islet of Raasay told me about her second cousin who spent all his time running the handle of a walking stick up and down the back of a cane chair; and periodically there would be a visiting preacher offering hell and damnation and other intoxi-cating joys, and following this orgy, there would always be a wee group of islanders led on to the boat on their way to Inverness. The town of Inverness is a pretty place, though cold and unfriendly for my own taste, but to the Hebrideans of a generation back, it was not a town at all, it was simply a lunatic asylum from which no traveller returned. It was only after I learned this in Stornoway that I could understand my own mother's feelings when she was discarded by her

The Red Cuillin,
from loch Sligachan,
Skye.

relatives as a girl, and packed off to domestic service in Inverness. It must have sounded like a one-way ticket to hell.

The great entertainment of the Highlands and the Islands is the ceilidh, because people can still sing with their own voices and find the energy to roister through the night when the mood is on them; and in a crowded kitchen with a drop or two now and then, there are few better ways to pass the night. The Highlander is a very rugged creature indeed. It's when the ceilidh leaves the kitchen and gets transplanted to a village hall that he needs his strength, and it's then that effete Lowlanders are wise to lie abed and read a book. At a formal Highland concert, including the mass concert-fest of the annual Mod, you need the stamina that sustains a trawlerman in a week-long gale. They go on forever, and the formal style of Highland singing is a sinister mock of the lilting Highland speech. It comes through the nose and every song has forty-two verses and it is an art form that requires the proper background, from birth, before it can be enjoyed or even tolerated. There was also a speciality act in the Stornoway district, an actual comedian, who turned up at every concert year after year, with an unchanging repertoire of jokes, every one written in a penny note-book so that none would ever be forgotten.

The macabre touch, I thought, was that he couldn't remember them himself, and after each joke, or even sometimes in the middle of a joke, he would sidle off the stage, consult the note-book, and then return with the next two lines of merry banter. But my refusal to be amused is certainly a sign of Lowland decadence. Nobody else minds at all.

The Uists are another set of islands with separate names and a geographical unity. North Uist, Benbecula and South Uist are physically joined so that you may be driven from one end to the other with dry feet. But it isn't hard to get wet in other ways. It was here that the *American Politician* was wrecked during the last war, loaded with export whisky, to inspire Compton Mackenzie's *Whisky Galore*, and the nonsense in the book is no more bizarre than the true stories. I myself, a temperate and careful man, was shambling drunk in the Uists at 10.30 a.m. and fell asleep on the heather with my face gaping at the sky in utter shamelessness.

That was nobody's fault but my own. At that time, and for many years previously, the Uists were blessed with the presence of Father John Morrison, the most turbulent priest of our day, who was always

Eilean Donan Castle, at the
foot of Loch Alsh

Inverness :
an old wife's tale

organising the island for some newsworthy ploy like demonstrating against the rocket bases and so on (another plot gifted to Compton Mackenzie on a plate) and *that* business had scarcely died away when somebody found a heap of unidentifiable teeth on one of the sandy beaches. Conforming to local custom, they were taken as everything was to Father John – it didn't matter whether a problem was discovered by a Catholic or a Protestant or a Muslim, Father John was the man for it because he was interested in absolutely everything.

The story filtered through to the mainland, without a moment's delay, that something pretty strange had been unearthed in the neighbourhood, possibly the remains of an extinct monster. Trilobites were mentioned, I recall, though not seriously, and the editor of the paper where I worked ordered me to write a high-level scientific analysis piece, blindfold, about the unerring accuracy of tests based on the half-life of radioactive carbon. This sounded so good that I found myself being bundled on to the BEA plane for Ben-becula the following morning to see the accursed things for myself.

I always have some inhibitions about bothering ministers of religion, especially of a religion which I have never shared, possibly from fear that they might convert me; but as soon as I telephoned Father Morrison he told me where to find a taxi and threw his doors open to me. The taxi was a creaking Dormobile with bits of farm machinery and oil and parcels for delivery all the way from Ben-becula to Lochboisdale in South Uist, and having engaged it for the day, I passed a dreamy hour travelling the delivery route till we got to the church house. I was led into a study at the back, madly cluttered with souvenirs and undeveloped films and books and half-opened packages of this and that, and the parish priest greeted me with delighted smiles. I never met a man who found more joy in living. He loved everything, and he didn't think much of his own theories about the strange teeth, but, as he explained, he was no expert and was merely theorising in a vacuum.

'And anyway,' he said, and laughed conspiratorially, and I knew I was in the conspiracy up to my neck, 'it adds to the gaiety of nations. I don't know that they're *not* prehistoric monster's teeth,' he added with a Jesuitical logic which I found irresistible. And while I was examining the fascinating specimens, which looked like over-sized melon seeds to me, he gave me the hospitality of the house in a frighteningly big tumbler. That is certainly one thing about Roman Catholic clergymen in Scotland: they take the solace of a good whisky for granted, whereas Protestant ministers will either shun it entirely or approach it with guilty defiance. I stood there, coldly analysing the teeth – they *were* teeth after all, on closer inspection – and thinking they looked rather fresh for prehistoric relics; and I stood there passing the time of day and many a jest with the happy humorous man who represented the Pope on the Uists. Then some English tourists came knocking at the door to ask for a look, and I went into the hall to telephone my paper with a rapid up-to-date story about the Great Uist Mystery. I did this with unfailing accuracy and fluency, never slurring a consonant, but as soon as I had laid down the telephone and my responsibilities were at an end, I realised I was miraculous drunk and gave way. I wandered out behind the house and found some heather and passed clean away till my taxi-driver came back from two of his deliveries and nudged me to move on to the next stop and have a drink.

They turned out to be the teeth of a basking shark in the end, I think.

The Uists, like many of the Hebridean islands, are treeless. Tall trunks can't stand the force of the naked Atlantic winds. The uplands are covered with stubborn shrubs and heather and bracken, and the coastal strip of machair, a fertile sandy soil, is cultivated for vegetables and feed. They are not the kind of islands men dream about when they imagine a life of eating the lotus and sunning the long days away.

They need tough people for survival; and however devious or alien they may seem to casual visitors, the islanders are tough and intensely human people. You may often suspect them and wonder at them but they and the islands have a charm that will lure you away from everything, if it gets time to work on you.

SCOTCH MIST

One autumn evening in the darkling, a solitary traveller might have been seen trudging through the glen of weeping, Glencoe, where murder and betrayal have glowered on the landscape since the bloody night the foul Campbells turned on their hosts the MacDonalds and murdered them as they slept. It is no place for a solitary traveller, especially one burdened with imagination, but the Youth Hostel still lay miles ahead and he tramped with nervous speed, for the mist that had caressed the high peaks all day was beginning to spread down towards the glen.

Even in bright daylight, in the comforting company of a coach-load of tourists, Glencoe clings to a darkness that is a part of the stones and the bracken. It is a place for respectful sorrow and quick departure. But as evening came down, so came the mist, and the single walker cursed it, but quietly, and put superstitious fear away from him. Even blind, he could hardly wander off the road, and warmth and friendly faces could not be far away. The mist thickened until he could scarcely see his own hand held before his face.

His senses jerked at a low swishing sound that came at him from behind out of the dark and he wheeled round with hammering heart, to breathe relief as he saw the two dim lights of a car slowly coming abreast of him. A motorist was worse off than himself, but at least he was human companionship, and the walker, a shy and courteous man in spite of the disquieting circumstances, called through the open window a nervous greeting which sounded out of place in his own ears. He was answered with a grunt that seemed to suggest invitation, and` as the machine crawled beside him, he opened the nearside door without expecting it to stop, and sat gingerly on the passenger seat with his pack on his knees. And there he sat for perhaps a minute, trying to think of something to say to his unspeaking host . . . until, as a vagrant puff of wind cleared a small patch of mist beside him, he was aware that there was no human face beside him in the gloom. Trying to seem too casual (for his own bene-fit rather than anyone else's) he moved his right hand towards the driver's seat, and a clammy sweat oozed on his forehead as the groping hand met nothing at all. There was no body beside him. But there was *something*. The pale blur of a human hand on the steering wheel, a hand that belonged to no body but gripped the wheel and slowly turned it this way and that.

Babbling silently to himself that it wasn't true, he stretched out to touch the ghostly hand. It started under his fingers and a sharp cry came from the darkness. The owner of the car was walking along the road, on the far side, pushing with one hand and steering with the other.

The Highland trails have their secret tales that would make your blood run cold (I misquote from that stout Scots Alaskan bard Robert W. Service). I know a nervous hill-walker who was also trapped by descending mist and found himself hours later, in solid darkness, lying along a rocky ledge with thin grass on top, in the sick knowledge that he had crawled out along a spur which might be any height at all, and which had come to a vertical end. Having no stick, he reached downwards all round with one hand, and then, trembling, with one foot, but never touched bottom. He composed himself to lie face down and wait for light. Light came, and he was lying on a dry stone dyke ten yards from a shepherd's cottage.

CHECK THAT
PLADDIE, LADDIE

The tartan is the great Scottish game, and it's a game in which anybody can join. It's funny to think that a length of woollen cloth with coloured squares on it can stir pride and passion in the heart of a nation, but it does; and of course it's a splendid lark and the envy of all lesser peoples like the Chinese, who are roused only by crude stimuli like the rice harvest and raw steel production.

Tartan is second only to whisky as an exportable element in Scottish culture. We have smothered chic women all over the world in yards of chromatic cloth, and lynx-eyed younger executives in California conceal checked underpants behind their smooth exteriors. A lot of this yardage is made in Austria or Hong Kong, it's true, but what the hell, it was our *idea*.

We also smile indulgent smiles at the strange and untraditional patterns adopted by well-meaning foreigners. These are not the true tartan, which adheres rigidly to certain designs laid down by God. They are what we genuine Scots call bum-bee tartans, from the fact that the bumble-bee has for centuries been trying to evolve into a Mackenzie, but like other foreigners has mixed up the warp with the woof.

We feel so strongly about tartan and its uses that, a few years ago, the Scottish nation finally rose in spluttering rage and abolished the spectacle of little girls competing as Highland dancers disguised as men, in velvet jackets, masculine kilts and tartan socks. These monsters increased their guilt by joggling up and down with all their past medals clinking on their little heaving bosoms, and honest Highlandmen fairly frothed at the sight. I loved it. It was wild.

The sword dancers

The reason for all this pious anger was that the kilt is an exclusively male outfit, divinely ordained since pre-Roman times. Some enthusiasts even believe that when the Roman legions reported those ancient Picts shambling about the Highlands dressed in nothing but paint, the paint was actually laid on in vertical and horizontal stripes, denoting the clan affiliation of the gentleman inside it.

It's quite true that tartan has a history, and it goes back farther than, say, the inverted gas mantle. It was capable of putting the fear of death in English governments in the eighteenth century, for instance.

In 1745, Charles Edward Stuart, Bonnie Prince Charlie, the Young Pretender, led his gallant Highlanders into the ludicrous blood-bath of Culloden, where English military discipline, the rifle and the bayonet vanquished the broadsword and the old clan system was smashed to hell. But it had been a close thing for a while, and the Government in London remained in a blind panic.

The Highlanders had been wearing their outlandish tartan suits, and since the Highlanders were weird beasts in the eyes of authority anyway, the tartan was taken to be a very big juju, heap strong totem, like Sioux war-bonnets, and the Government realised it could shear the Scotsman of his courage by abolishing the stuff altogether. A law was passed in 1746 forbidding the wearing of multi-coloured cloths in the Highlands. Penalty for the first offence, six months in jail; for a second offence, seven years' transportation to the Colonies. A few rash Highlanders were actually nabbed for this fiendish crime.

But peace finally filtered into the Highlands, and the law was repealed in 1782, because by this time Scotchness was suddenly becoming fashionable again. Sir Walter Scott, good man, had started to glorify the old legends of Rob Roy MacGregor and such-like, and when George IV paid his state visit to Edinburgh in 1822, tartan broke out like measles everywhere. If you didn't have tartan, boy, you were nothing. The King himself wore a kilt, and a braw spectacle he made, if you had a macabre sense of humour. Walter Scott himself stage-managed this Edinburgh frenzy, and he was completely hipped on the tartan.

He had seen the effect it could have on innocent strangers when he went to Paris during the occupation after Waterloo, and he noted that 'the singular dress of our Highlanders makes them particular objects of attention to the French'. I'll bet.

The Emperor of Russia was taken with the lads too. At his par-

ticular request, a sergeant, a corporal and a private soldier of a
Highland regiment paraded before him secretly at the Elysee Palace,
and the Emperor, who had heard strange tales, achieved an ambition
which is still nursed by nosey-parkers all over the world today. He
lifted Sergeant Thomas Campbell's kilt to see if it was true that there
was nothing below.

By that time, of course, the Great Kilt Nonsense was well established. The kilt was the kilt pretty much as we see it today; an enormous length of tartan pleated across the back, and with the pleats
stitched together at the top, and with the unpleated end bits laid one
above the other across the front. We go mad for this today, if we have
the courage, or if we have conveniently emigrated to some place
where we can impress the natives. The kilt is a fine swaggering garment, and as far as function goes, it is at least as rational as those
newfangled trouser things.

I bought my first kilt when I was fifteen, and had a rough time
defending it against my purist acquaintances because it was a Gordon, and there have never been any Gordons in my lineage. The
explanation is quite simple. The Gordon was the only kilt I could get
for three quid.

If I had been rich, I would have ordered a MacLean by right of
my maternal grandmother. This is what we do when we're rich and
meticulous. No man is entitled to wear a tartan except the family
tartan he has inherited. The tartan shops have charts and books with
all the official patterns listed, and all the thousands of names that can
claim to be branches or septs or chums of the great tartan clans. It is
a splendid piece of hokum.

In that battle of Culloden, the Highlanders wore any tartan that
came up their backs. They had never heard of the idea of an official
clan design, and if they had, they would have dodged it because in
those days advertising your name could easily get you a dirk between
the ribs. The old clansmen recognised their friends in battle by
wearing cockades or bits of feather or familiar expressions.

The kilt they wore wasn't a badge of office, it was a travelling
tent incorporating instant camouflage. The best pattern was one
that would merge into the scenery. The garment itself was a
length of woollen cloth, two yards by six yards, which I admit sounds
ridiculous but is no dafter than a sari. At night, the clansman wrapped
himself in it and slept. In the morning, he laid a belt on the ground
and then carefully pleated the great lump of stuff on top of the belt.

And then – yes, I know it sounds like a music-hall act, but it was strictly business – he lay down on top of the lot, brought the ends of the belt up, and buckled it round his waist. He was now enclosed in a tube of cloth, reaching from his knees to right over his head.

He then stood up, breathing heavily, and taking the upper end of his cocoon in both hands, he did the best he could with it, possibly with a pin or two or the odd knot. He was now formidably insulated against cold and wet and could run like a rabbit. After the thing was banned in 1746, years passed and the Highlander went off the notion. It took Walter Scott and the 'bon ton' of Edinburgh to put the kilt back in the hit parade.

And now we come to the two brothers of Albanie, and one of the nicest confidence tricks of modern times. The brothers went by various names, and in fact, they changed their names every few years, but they are best remembered as Sobieski Stuart (John and Charles). They were a handsome pair, of great charm and artistic sensibility, and wherever they had come from, they landed in Edinburgh at the right historical moment. The tartan frenzy was still rollicking along, after all that excitement with George IV and that prying Russian Emperor, and the boys gave it out that their father had told them that they were grandsons of Bonnie Prince Charlie himself. Who knows? Charlie was always up to *something*.

Both brothers were slick hands at wood-carving and other high-toned pursuits. They spent a lot of their time as house guests, and one of their hostesses, who liked them but was no fool, once noticed that John had taken a great fancy to a tartan bedspread in the house. Any minute now he'll be wearing it, she told a friend. Almost instantly, he turned up wearing it. Not only that, he had created a history for it. Ah, good old John.

I like to think of the glorious turmoil in his brain at that moment. Wood-carving was all very well, but he had suddenly found a place in history, because he was going to write history with himself in the middle of it. Pretty soon he was able to announce that he was in possession of a Latin manuscript setting forth the forgotten and the only true patterns of the clan tartans. Edinburgh started coming to the boil. Walter Scott, it's true, was very leery about the whole story. It sounded like a good gag to him, but he wanted to have a look at the original manuscript, whose Latin sounded pretty dubious at second-hand. John Sobieski Stuart couldn't bring himself to endanger the precious paper by parting with it, but he now claimed he had collated it against another manuscript 'in the Augustine Monastery in Cadiz.'

And in 1842, the boys published their *Vestiarium Scoticum*, settling the clan tartans for good. It was published by William Tait of Edinburgh, and it was a rave. Everybody, of course, wanted in on the act. Families who hadn't even had a pair of knees now discovered they had a tartan, all to themselves.

'It is well known,' said Sir John Sinclair in 1830, 'that the Philibeg (short kilt) was invented by an Englishman in Lochaber about 60 years ago.' Who wants killjoys like Sinclair going about robbing us of our heritage? Such moaners didn't have a chance against the Sobieski Stuarts. Heavens above, John Sobieski Stuart was the *Comte d'Albanie*. He said so himself.

And so we Scots have the kilt, and what's more, we have our *own* kilt, and if we are MacTooshers, no MacPoosher can insult us by flaunting our tartan above his traitorous knees. And the kilt, designed by Providence, changeth not, it developeth not, and is nice. Trousers get narrower, jackets get shorter, shirts get drippier, and coats adapt themselves to the swinging rhythm of time. But the kilt is immutable and we love it and we will defend it to the end. We won't wear it, but we'll defend it.

THE LONG WALK

Some years ago, everybody started talking about a daunting middle-aged lady, Dr Barbara Moore, who appeared to live on honey and her own conversation, and walked single-handed from John o' Groats to Land's End. This infuriated many people with legs, and several of them travelled to John o' Groats to show that they could do the same thing faster, or backwards, or pushing peas with their noses. For a while it looked as if long-distance walking might oust bigamy as a national sport. It didn't happen, of course, but it was touch and go at the time.

At first, the field was left open to athletes and specialised maniacs, but when Billy Butlin announced that he would give real cash money for the winner of a walking race the length of Britain, one realised that amazing scenes would be witnessed. Road, rail and air services to the north were jammed as the British public moved in for the easiest thousand pounds ever offered. There were nearly as many reporters and photographers as there were competitors, and the newspaper I worked for had the brilliant notion that I should not merely report the fun, but get right in among it, on my feet. It sounded fine, and precisely fitted my philosophy that Anybody Can Do Anything. I started reading *Scouting for Boys* and experimenting with thick socks and thin socks and socks full of talcum powder, and underwear made of knotted rope.

I was not underestimating the grimness of the task. Though fit and sinewy and well-shaped when I pulled in my paunch, I had been out of competitive sport for some little time. My usual form of invigorating exercise was a careful stroll across a hotel lounge and a quick tomato juice. I wasn't too sure about shoes and boots either, but I went into training at once, trying out my stock of footwear on alternative evenings and walking as much as two miles with my chest thrown out and my eye on the money. There was snow on the ground.

Sanity intervened, and for the sake of my professional commitments, I decided that I wouldn't go the whole distance and cheat some genuine enthusiast of the prize. I would walk only halfway, or part way, to get the atmosphere of the thing. In fact, I would walk from John o' Groats to Wick, which is all of nineteen miles. And then I would still be available to write a sizzling story of How It Felt. Nobody laughed at this. The kind of people I know do not sneer at a walk of nineteen miles.

I still think it's a pity Mr Butlin didn't stick in and make the mass walk an annual fest, because nobody in Caithness, or the newspaper business, has ever seen anything like it in history. The snow was still on the ground up there, and at Renfrew Airport numbers of frantic reporters were trying to bribe their way on to crowded planes to be there on time. In dead of winter, the hotels in far-off Wick were bulging with free-spending custom and the wee shops were praying for rapid delivery of gumboots and corn plasters and aspirin for the biggest bonanza of all time. Although the air was as cold as a scalpel, the streets were humming with people all glowing with hysteria. The natives were hysterical too – and not only from the sight of so much dough pouring in. Up in Wick, they *liked* us. The Caithness folk, whom I had never met before, fairly shine with simple kindness. With snow added, it felt like the Klondyke, but without the killing fever.

Every few minutes of the day and night, straggling prospectors were finding their way in. Scout halls and drill halls and church halls were opened as dormitories. A sad, shifty little woman turned up at my hotel to ask for a temporary job as a waitress in order to grubstake her entry for the Walk. She agreed that she wouldn't be a very fast waitress because she suffered horrible with her feet. A slim young man was observed trying out his legs in a morning suit with top hat and cane. The newspaper gang positively had the Klondyke feeling. Wick was a million miles from home, it was impossible *not* to get plenty of stories, and nobody at head-office could have any idea how much bribe-money it was costing. Hard-eyed blokes from *The People* or *The Mirror* were exchanging brotherly quips with

gentlemen from *The Times* newspaper. Improbable, nubile young women, who must have been starlets looking for a break, were being plied with dry Martinis and interviewed in dark corners.

On the day of the Walk, Wick began to empty in a panic. It was still nineteen miles to the starting line, and the long narrow road was strung out with terror-stricken hitch-hikers and taxis and trucks. There isn't much at John o' Groats except a hotel and a few buildings and that multi-sided folly that John built. I never expect to see it again, because it wouldn't look the same without Billy Butlin's marquee and a mob of lunatics spilling everywhere. The sun shone in the middle of the day. John o' Groats is really the end of the line. Across the water to the north was the island of Stroma, brown-red in the sunlight and waiting for a buyer. I thought it might be nice to buy it, if I could move it somewhere else. A man from the *News of the World* offered me a slug from his pocket flask, and I recoiled in horror at the idea of competing half-sloshed, and took one.

There was a tubby little American, wearing pince-nez fastened to his hat by a chain, and a cellophane cover on his hat. He didn't believe in socks, and wore toeless sandals with polythene wrapped round his toes to keep them dry. He had a bundle of papers under his arm, and he was entering the walk to vindicate his disagreement with Einstein, whom he regarded as a good man but misguided.

'I have proved,' he told us, 'that e is not equal to mc squared, but to mc cubed.' Seven or eight reporters were crowded round him shouting questions into the wind and taking notes.

'What the hell is MCQ?' one of them asked me, because I was known to be a scientific fake.

'It's some kind of photographic developer,' I said happily. The other reporter wasn't walking 19 miles that night, and therefore deserved no quarter. There was a woman in high-heeled shoes, with a brown coat and a pixie hood, and a string bag containing enough groceries to last for 500 miles. She walked about bent over to one side to balance the groceries. A girl was entering in a bathing costume. There were walkers in track suits and walkers in running shorts. Another woman was proposing to push a pram to the south of England. A syndicate had a trek cart loaded with their safari supplies. There were family parties spanning the generations. Somewhere down the road, Mr Butlin had an ambulance in wait to pick up collapsers. He knew what he was doing.

But in its crazy way it was magnificent. Three-quarters of the walkers had a slim hope of getting back to Wick on their feet, never mind Land's End. They were mad. They had no right to be getting in the way. But even if it's not true that Anybody Can Do Anything, it stuck out a mile that anybody could *try* anything. There were so many loons in for the race that it was hard to tell when it actually started. Humanity surged back and forth aimlessly till the news got through the crowd, and by that time the early birds were pounding down the road into the distance.

By then I had worked out the secret strategy. Since I wasn't going to finish the race, I didn't need to reserve my effort, and therefore, just for fun, I would be in the first rank of starters and run like hell all the way to Wick.

The honour of my newspaper, of my native city, of my family, was at stake. I and no other would be first past the Wick checkpoint, and *then* collapse.

What a pathetic fool I was. By the time I wormed my way through the tortoise group, the leader of the pack must have been two miles away, and these boys in front were no dilettantes. They meant to win, and they were the kind of tough-muscled swine who would tear off twenty miles to warm up for a sprint.

Still, it was possible to be in the first ten. Fifty? Hundred? Darkness started to come down almost at once. It was now clear why the clever lads had got off early. Inside half-an-hour, it was nearly impossible to jostle through the procession at the rear. And for the first time, the old competitive curse of humanity was beginning to show. The slow walkers had set themselves a timetable, and they were sticking to it to maintain their strength, but you could tell that they hated anybody who overtook them. The farther they walked, the more they hated the overtakers. The reality of those hundreds of miles must have been starting to loom at last. Most of them walked in groups, each forming a phalanx, so that to overtake you had to scramble into the packed snow at the roadside; and very soon, there was no polite giving way. We all had the lust for gold.

After three miles, walking alone, too quickly, in the dark, on a road crowded with hostile strangers, I developed the conviction that the leaders must be away across the English border. I stuck to my plan of walking a hundred, running a hundred. It was all right, except for the occasional sight of other reporters swishing along in hired cars to look at us, and probably swigging from hip-flasks the while, and me not even in a position to justify any expenses till I got back to Wick.

One good thing happened. Halfway between John o' Groats and Wick there's a completely meaningless village called Keiss. I'm not trying to knock the place, it's only that I couldn't see any reason why it was there at all. Maybe it looks logical in summer, but at that time of year it baffled all conjecture. You might as well have put up an antique shop bang in the middle of Antarctica for all the sense it made. And it wasn't just a huddle of wee rustic cottages. It was a street of *tenements*. With street lamps. I looked it up yesterday in the atlas, and it's there all right. I had begun to wonder if the whole experience was a mirage caused by the Aurora Borealis. Anyway, what happened was that we all came shambling one by one out of the northern darkness into this main street and found the whole population of the district lined up on both sides to offer a rousing welcome to each and every fool. And this audience wasn't even walking or running, it was standing there, freezing to death and managing to radiate goodwill. I got stage fright. It's one thing staggering through a desert landscape and feeling gormless, but you know the feeling when you're up to something private and absurd and suddenly the stage-manager switches on the lights and there's a packed house out there all the time. I swerved off the road and tried to sneak down the pavement behind the crowd, hoping they would think I was an innocent householder who had nipped out to buy a tin of condensed milk. This was a total failure.

They could probably tell by the outfit that I wasn't a legitimate resident. I was togged up – and now I come to think of it, these little details of walkers' techniques should not be omitted – in what I have found by experiment to be the ideal set for physical heroism: Checked sports jacket by Maxie Mann of Sauchiehall Street; Daks trousers; shirt, socks and cellular underwear by Marks and Spencer; string gloves by Copland and Lye; cotton showerproof by Swallow; tie by Munrospun; black leather, crepe-soled Flotillas by Clarks. I still have the shoes. Sometimes in thoughtful moments I take them out and kick them round the living-room. I could have walked into any Mecca ballroom without raising an eyebrow. Up in Keiss, I managed to get the whole crowd on the west side of Main Street to turn their backs on the road and pat me on the back as I slithered along the pavement. They had been keeping count, too. 'You're fine, lad,' they shouted, 'There's only a hundred and eighteen in front of you.'

I suppose they cheered with as much enthusiasm for Number 800. These Caithness characters just don't wear out.

South of Keiss, it went all quiet and black and horrible again. Let us draw a veil, for God's sake. About two miles short of Wick, another of those reporter thugs drew alongside me in a black Citroen, and I snarled quietly and tottered away till I realised he was hanging out of the window and calling me by name. It was my own photographer, a splendid Christian gentleman who had come out to persuade me to betray my trust by taking a lift, and while I was wrestling with my conscience and dragging the car door open, another hiker drew alongside and crumpled up unconscious on the roadside. Oh boy, I loved that man. We couldn't do anything else but lift him into the Citroen and rush him to hospital, with me to hold his hand. It wasn't all that funny, in fact. The unknown walker was as pale as snow, and for a minute or two I thought he had died in my lap. But they took him in cheerfully at the hospital and warmed him up and we went down to the hotel in Wick.

The man from *The Times* newspaper had just wandered out from the bar, drinking a large whisky, and he greeted me with a gesture that nearly convinced me of English supremacy. He rammed his own drink into my hand.

'Rather a newsy weekend,' he said affably, and I gulped and said yes. Then I said, 'To what news are you referring to which?' and I had one of those pricklings of the scalp that folk get in tough detective stories.

'Princess Margaret's got engaged,' he said patiently. 'Hadn't you heard?'

'God!' I said. 'She couldn't have waited another day!'

'It's handy for the Sundays,' he argued. There was no harm in the man at all. He was taking a balanced view of the situation. But who was going to want to read about heroic reporters walking through endless Caithness nights when a whole princess was available? With my life in ruins, I fell asleep over a dish of stewed steak and went to bed. A lassie came and slipped five or six hot water bottles in beside me and I went into a three-day coma. This was interrupted two hours later by MacNicol, a dangerous feature-writer from *The Express*, with the news that a hospital matron was throwing a late-night party, so I leapt from bed in a clatter of mangled bones and we whooped it up till three or four. We had to walk home too, and it rained.

THE ORANGE
AND THE GREEN

So there was this fella that went into a pub near Ibrox Park, and he has an alligator walking beside him on a lead, and he says to the barman, 'Here, mac, do you serve Catholics in this pub?' So naturally the boys might have been annoyed in the normal way, but they didny fancy the look of this alligator, and they kept well back and looked respectful, and the barman says, 'Sure, sirr, it's quite all right,' so the man says, 'Aye, right, a pint for me and a Catholic for my pal here.'

And then there was this other fella on a Saturday night bus to Castlemilk, and he thought the fare was sixpence, but the Pakistani conductor says it was eightpence, so they argued the toss for a while because the fella had a good bucket in him, but he finally paid up, but here, as the Pakistani was walking back down the bus, the fella turns round and shouts, 'Away, ya durty Orange get!'

There was also these two Rangers supporters that went to the Odeon to see *Quo Vadis*, and Charlie says to Hughie, 'Here, I'll have to get out, these Christians getting mutilated and flung to lions and that, I can never stand cruelty, it makes my blood curdle.' But Hughie says, 'Sit down there, you've paid your money, and anyway, in these days all the Christians were Catholics.' So Charlie peers at the screen again, and says, 'Hey, what's that lion supposed to be up to, sittin' there doin' *nothin*'?'

Then there was the drunk man standing on the parapet of the Stockwell Bridge, and a crowd collected, and he said he was for committing suicide, so a kind-hearted man went up to him and said, 'I know you've got your troubles, but stop, for the sake of your family.' 'I've got no family.' 'All right, then, for the sake of the good old Rangers.' 'I don't support Rangers.' 'Okay, well,' says the man, 'I'm not prejudiced. For the sake of *Celtic*.' 'I don't support Celtic either,' says this bloke on the bridge. 'Right, Jump, ya rotten atheist!'

I once took two American jazzmen into Denholm's Bar, just down the street from the Glasgow Central Hotel, and they said they loved Scotland because they had just come from Texas, and it was a delight to be in a country where nobody gave a damn about a man's colour.

'I accept your compliment on behalf of my native country,' I said with old-world courtesy, 'and you'll be fine as long as you keep your mouth shut about religion.' They laughed like anything. At least religion doesn't *show*.

It doesn't, either, because I've tried out the Glasgow theory that you can tell a Catholic by looking at him. What kind of a city would develop a superstition like that?

Come to think of it, I suppose Birmingham, Alabama, could do exactly the same thing. The more I think of it, in fact, the more I realise that we don't shoot people in the back in Glasgow or set fire to them because they have the wrong colour or the wrong religion. We only throw bottles now and then, and only under stress of deep emotion, as when the Protestant Rangers are playing the Catholic Celtic at a game derisively described as football. But you can live all your life in Scotland without ever going to see Celtic and Rangers, and this is the way most people in Scotland plan their lives.

It's the lousy old history that accounts for religious feuding in the West of Scotland, naturally. We blame the whole thing on the Irish, a notably convenient people for blaming things on. The Irish started everything. The name Scot was imported to this country by a wandering tribe from Ireland, the Scoti, who immediately started feuding with the local Picts, or Picti (the people who wore blue paint) and since those days we have never been short of an excuse for another punch-up. In the nineteenth century, the British Government was faced with the Irish potato famine, and by exercise of thought and ingenuity, succeeded in converting this into a national disaster which cut back the population by two million. Some of the Micks who still had the strength to stagger to the coastal towns and sixpence left for boat-fare, fled to Scotland and set up a minority problem. By that time, thanks to John Knox and other stubborn

Glasgow: an Orange Walk

subversives, Scotland had gone Protestant, and the Irish immigrants were all hot and strong for Popery. They went in for mumbo-jumbo with crucifixes and painted idols, and this was viewed with panic suspicion not only by native Scotsmen, but by other immigrants from Ireland who had fought with William of Orange to put down the Irish Catholic Rebellion some time before – or who *would* have fought with King Billy, if it had been convenient.

Some of the Catholic immigrants had joined a foul secret society, the Fenians, dedicated to the independence of Ireland, and pretty soon every Catholic of any nationality was known positively to be a treasonous Fenian. That's how it all started, and the top witch-hunters were Irish-oriented Protestants of the Orange movement, an interesting historical society which holds a big Walk every year and takes a dram in the name of religious purity.

Most of the time, you never notice this at all, but occasionally you have to tread a thin line. I was coming out of Tom's Bar one day with Jimmy Donnelly, the crime reporter of the Glasgow *Evening Citizen*, and we were talking about something very high-toned, like Kierkegaard or the *Kama Sutra*, something intellectual like that, when a jovial member of the artisan classes approached silently from behind and patted us both on the back and said,

'Aye, us crowd has to stick thegither, eh?'

'Eh?' we said.

'Ach, you know, boys?' And he made a stylish drop-kick movement *with the left foot*. That's a sure sign, you see. Catholics kick with the left foot.

'Aye, sure,' we said, which is the formula for avoiding any trouble in Glasgow no matter what anybody has said. And we parted with furtive thumbs-up signals.

'He thinks the pair of us are Fenian gets,' Jimmy said to me, and my amiable features turned stern.

'That's all right for you,' I said. 'You *are* a Fenian get.' The trouble with me is the name Hanley, which was brought from County Roscommon two generations back and can label a man. It was brought by a devout Catholic too, but the faith sort of diluted itself as the generations went on till it reached me as Calvinism and left me as nothing at all. Mind you, life was always dangerous around a man like Donnelly, who has an earnest chubby face and means no harm whatever, but can attract crises like a magnet. When he wrote a kindly piece about the death of the last of the Protestant gangsters, the king of the Billy Boys, he started getting anonymous phone calls, threatening him with death, and this is even more remarkable since he didn't have a telephone at the time. One day I was out in the city with Donnelly, going about lawful occasions, in company with another Irish-sounding thug, Brian Feeny, a history teacher who keeps playing the piano and singing 'In the Good Old Summer Time' and who in spite of the name is a strictly non-Pope man, and everything happened to Donnelly that can happen to a man who is minding his own business. First of all we went into a bookshop and Donnelly picked three Penguins and paid for them, but Feeny and I were still browsing and he came back in to wait for us. On the way out, an assistant ran round the counter and accused Donnelly of trying to steal three paperbacks. It did no good when Feeny and I backed up his claim that he had paid for them – we were obviously a large-scale criminal outfit, and they had to fetch the manageress to adjudicate, and she didn't believe us either. She let us go because she didn't want the shop wrecked.

Brooding, we went round to a pub in Hope Street and Feeny and I kept patting Jimmy on the back and telling him *we* knew he was an honest man. All the time a stranger at the far end of the bar kept trying to catch my eye, and I turned on my glassy stare and I looked past him, and Jimmy said he was an obvious moocher. No sooner had the words been spoken than this moocher's mate materialised at our elbows, grabbed Jimmy by the arm, and said,

'Are you sneerin' at my pal?'

Donnelly, already embittered by fate, threw the stranger's arm off, but people in pubs get very persistent, and this one was looking for retribution.

'Right, outside!' he snarled. Outside, I ask you – in the middle of a main street at ten past five. Donnelly was blowing twin jets of steam down his nostrils, and, acting as his friends, we elbowed the stranger aside and urged him away from the trouble area.

'You would think I had the evil eye or something,' Jimmy said bitterly, glaring at the traffic in Hope Street, and dead on cue, a Morris Minor passed under his nose and its front nearside wheel fell right off.

One night in Barcelona, on a secret mission, I fell into the company of a middle-aged doctor from New York State who was doing the grand tour on his own, being a widower. His name was Edwin Shea, and for want of anybody more fascinating, we joined up for

Tenements: Maryhill Glasgow

the evening, and I may say we got clipped for eleven quid for buying four Coca-Colas for two lassies in a night-club, so don't tell me anything about the low cost of living in Spain. However, Ed would have no part in this narrative except that he visited Glasgow on his way home and I picked him up at noon one Saturday to buy him a cheap nasty lunch. He was in a condition of bewilderment because he had spent the morning failing to get through the crowds in a city which he had always thought to be old, folksy and quiet. It only then dawned on me that this agreeable Catholic foreigner had somehow picked the day of the Orange Walk to be in Glasgow, and not only that, he was due to sail for Ireland the same night. In his place, I would have simulated appendicitis and stayed underground till the following week, but these Americans are tough travellers, hungry for experience.

On the day of the Orange Walk, the native enthusiasts are swollen by a really fervent contingent which comes over from Ulster, the home of Orangery, and those of them who are sober enough to find the dock, travel back to Ulster on the same night. Doctor Shea got his cheap lunch and we exchanged some corn, and then he vanished from human ken temporarily, but I had a letter from him in America describing the educational night he had spent on the Belfast boat, listening to the songs and thuds through the thin walls of his cabin and making rapid diagnoses all night as limbs scrunched on companionways and stomachs were hurled into the Irish Sea, and then covering his face with the blankets and possibly praying, for all I know. He complained philosophically that he had ended up minus a new camera which he had bought in Italy, and I wrote him a brusque note advising him to be thankful, and telling him to count his fingers, toes and heads if he didn't agree with me.

THE NOAKER

When it comes to buying property, Noaker Todd used to say, the best thing is to fit your money into a launching ramp and fling it at the moon; then at least you'll be able to see it on a clear night. Noaker is also the man who in a philosophical moment remarked that as one door closes, that's the time to jam your boot in it.

Noaker never existed, I made him up. At least, I *think* I made him up, at a time when I was trying to exorcise the horrid fascination the Glasgow tenements always had for me. But the longer I went on about Noaker and his chip-loving family in the Toonheid district of Glasgow, the more I feared that I was being used as an automatic writer. I found myself talking like Louie the Lodger, the gay bachelor man-about-town railway clerk, who occupied the Todd's front room in a state of hypnotised fear. Louie is, I mean Louie was, addicted to a prissy form of English prose, like many Glaswegians when they want to make a serious point, and he never *complained*, but always *remonstrated*, about the Noaker's proclivity for purloining coin of the realm from gas-meters. He also clings, I mean clung, to a lavendery obsolete short-story convention, like this.

I had long been curious regarding the early life of my landlord Mr Noaker Todd, but I never liked to seem too inquisitive about it, because I have a natural sense of delicacy about asking questions that may get me a punch on the ear.

How, for instance, had the Noaker graduated into a system of life from which legitimate employment was rigorously excluded? A way of life which nevertheless was almost legal, what's more? (He has not been in the pokey, even on a ten-day stretch for, oh, a couple of years at least).

I was therefore suddenly galvanised into attention when, one evening in Donnelly's Bar, the Noaker abruptly burst out into a recital of his last Big Job.

'Ach, the biggest job you ever done was one a these automatic mulk machines,' said Ned, the charge-hand, a character of brutal cynicism where the Noaker is concerned.

The Noaker smiled quietly, dead superior, and picked up his pint fast because among those present was numbered Charlie Crum, the Toonheid Tealeaf, who makes other people's pints vanish by a system of yogi, or something.

Charlie, who had been scanning the bar and counting the fittings to see if any might be detachable, looked wistful as Big Ned proceeded to fasten the O A P Holiday Fund collection box to the counter with four-inch screws.

'Jist figure to yourselves,' the Tealeaf said in a dream, 'figure to yourselves, knockin' off a billion trillion pounds in gold bullion in a wanny. That's the kinda job I always wanted. You get awful fed up stealin' mangles an' auld tram-rails.' Something in the man's frank dishonesty moved me, because in spite of his single-minded dedication to thieving, the Tea was constantly being lumbered with articles like decayed tank-traps which had no market value in any pawnshop within a mile of Toonheid.

'I was only seventeen when we done a bank,' the Noaker said airily, and amid groans of disbelief he flicked the ash off his fag into Charlie's pint and stared back into his past.

'It was real big-time, none of your brick-through-a-windae stuff,' he said, and then seemed to grope for details. 'It was the war that done it — you know, the horrors a battle workin' on the psychological balance of men's minds, an' that. Flanders, Wypers, Mespot, ach, it was sickenin'.'

'You mean Wypers' pub?' Ned asked callously. The Noaker paid him no heed.

'Of course, I was only a boay — a mere boay, it's criminal when you think aboot it,' he continued. Charlie Crum, his brain lumbering at a terrible pace to keep track, asked humbly, 'Did you see much fightin'?'

'Fightin'?' the Noaker hooted. 'Fightin'? The Army hardly took time to issue me wi' a pair a left-fitted boots before they had me

ements :
Townhead . Glasgow

posted tae Edinburgh Castle, an' intae battle straight away. I got punched stupit in every pub in Rose Street inside a week. Don't interrupt, will you?

'So there we wur, battered an' senseless wi' the viciousness of war, crawlin' alang Princes Street on hauns an' knees, when some eedjit blew the Armistice, and we got flung intae civilian life like rats in a trap.

'Personally, me myself, I would probably have moved intae industry or commerce, or shovin' a barra or somethin' scunnersome, but there was a bloke in this unit – you've heard aboot the Mad Major? Big-time gentleman crook? Well, this guy was the Loony Lieutenant. Educatit, an' everythin' – he had went to three public schools at the same time – but war had turned him intae a enemy a society. He had got punched stupit in Rose Street as well.'

'Jist like the telly!' Charlie Crum breathed in stupefied admiration, and the Noaker glared at him with a guilty start.

'Will you zipp the gub a minute and let me try an' mind the story?' he demanded. 'So, as I was elucidatin', this Loony Lieutenant had a great scheme to get back at the world for givin' him a chip on his shooder an' two broken teeth. In nae time he had collected a crowd a hand-picked men.

'We were a' young, an' brave as anythin', an' we would have went through a fire for the Lieutenant, as long as it was unlit. He ran the entire thing like a military operation.'

'You mean he loused it up?' asked Ned, who had been gripped against his will by the Noaker's reminiscences.

'I will be compelled for to move intae a pub where the staff don't ram their big illiterate noses intae gentlemen's conversations,' the Noaker complained. 'You jist keep the pints comin', that's your job, it's your round, Louie, isnit?'

I have noticed on previous occasions how adroitly it always contrives to be my round, but I accept that life must take its toll in Donnelly's Bar.

'So,' the Noaker continued, 'before we were so iggerantly interrupted, there we wur, trained tae a split second. First thing, the Lieutenant borrowed some money aff this auld auntie that owned a big estate by the name of Yorkshire, an' he set up in business as a fancy interior decorator. This, you may interject, is hardly a good-goin' criminal enterprise aimed at the heart a society, but ours was not for to reason why.

'So we a' learned for to work the auld whitewash brushes an' that, an' got nice white dungarees, tae make it look good. Tell you the truth, we had tae stick at that for aboot eight months before the Lieutenant was able to arrange Phase Two of the operation – distemperin' a bank!'

The fiendish cunning of this jolted Charlie so much that he swallowed his pint the wrong way, and had to whip up my pint and drink it before he recovered.

'Now then,' said the Noaker. 'There's folk workin' in the bank, see? So they don't like their customers gettin' distempered while they're depositin' their fourpences. So you gotty work at the week-end, see?

'Right enough, there was always a bank bloke there alang wi' us, but it was only a holiday for him. We plied him wi' cigarettes tae keep him cheery while the eight of us flung the distemper here an' there. But naturally we had tae keep makin' tea, an' the plumbing supplies were in the cellar, get it?

'So there was always two or three of the crowd doonstairs clashin' the pans, as it were, but actually chisellin' a hole through the brickwork.'

There fell a pregnant silence, broken only by the click of Charlie

Crum's nails as his hand inched towards an unoccupied pint. The Noaker struggled as with some terrible memory before he could go on.

'You see, the Lieutenant had the entire thing worked oot. He had drew maps an' everything. He was loony, mind you, but like yon mad geniuses, they're a' a bit touched in the heid. Everything had to be rehearsed like a ballet dance. He even *bought* a brick wall for us to practise knockin' holes in it during the week.'

'Hey, *that's* clever!' Big Ned agreed, sweating with curiosity and ramming his cigarette in Charlie Crum's hand to discourage him. 'But you got caught, I bet you you got caught, eh? They always get caught.'

'Kindly demonstrate a modicum of forbearance while we are tore up internally wi' traumatic recollections, you iggerant big get,' said the Noaker. 'Not a bit. We were too fly for that. Listen, we had got every angle covered. This was a genuine operation planned by a master-mind. Come the Sunday night, a wee fella, Snitch, came up the stairs covered in blue distemper an' brick dust, an' whispered tae the Lieutenant that the breakthrough was completed.

'Quick as a flash, the Lieutenant gave the bank guy a cuppa tea, loaded wi' some drug unknown tae medical science – cascara, I think – an' the lotty us belted doon these stairs an' through the hole. We could hear the bank guy screamin' at the telephone, which I may add, we had put the wires through a mincer, anyway, an' we had five minutes tae load up, heave the stuff on our horse an' cairt, an' away to the South Seas at a dinger. It worked like cloakwork. We were away roon four corners before the bank guy managed tae ram his skull through the front door and scream Polis.'

'Oh, fantastic,' Charlie Crum breathed. 'How much did youse get, Noaker?'

'How much did we get?' Noaker's voice was impatient with contempt. 'How much do you think we would get, knockin' a hole through a bank cellar?' And he paused and passed a trembling hand over his brow. 'The hole led straight through to the sweetie-shop cellar next door. The horse an' cairt was gallopin' through Bathgate by the time we discovered we had got away wi' 50,000 Crunchy Bars an' two jars a black-striped balls.'

'But it was the bank you were supposed to be crackin',' Big Ned protested.

'Aye, aye, *I* know that, an' *you* know that. We should have got a

job distemperin' the sweetie-shop. But as I have already telt you, this Lieutenant was loony. He had just been readin' the map upside-doon, maybe.

'An' yet, I don't know. You should have saw him gorgin' these Crunchy Bars. He had a terrible sweet tooth. Maybe, in his dementit way, he was achieving his destiny.'

There was a deep, baffled silence in Donnelly's Bar, during which everybody turned to stare at me, and I caught on and ordered another round.

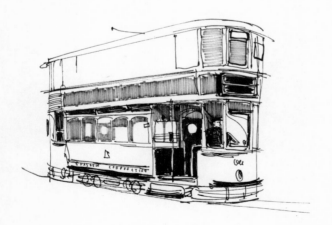

THE GRADE-MAKERS

Every Scottish schoolchild grows up in the happy knowledge that Scotsmen invented everything worth having, in the same way as every Russian tot discovers that Shakespeare and Leonardo were not only Russians, but premature Bolsheviks. According to Oliver Brown, of whom more in a minute, Byron and Ruskin and Macaulay were Scots under the skin, because no Englishman could have been as original as any of them. Our one solid religious dogma is that a Scotsman will succeed where all others fail.

Well, it's the truth anyway. The only reason why traitors like me keep knocking Scotland is that the place is so flaming marvellous that it embarrasses us to talk about it in plain fact. Considering the size of the place, and the number of political tricks that have been pulled on the country in modern times, and the permanent economic crisis, and all those futile unploughable mountains, and the rain, (or maybe because of all those things) Scotsmen have kept revolutionising everything. Even a cursory list is fairly frightening. It was the Scotsman Napier who invented logarithms, the Scotsman Simpson who launched the science of anaesthesia by applying chloroform, the Scotsman MacMillan who built the first decent bicycle (he came from Dumfries, and the minute he cycled into Glasgow he was arrested on a breach-of-the-peace charge for riding to the danger of the lieges); it was Black who discovered latent heat, and Clerk Maxwell who made wireless possible, Baird who invented television, Watson Watt who devised Radar and Fleming who led the research in penicillin.

The Scots are a fantastic people. Perched in a corner of real

estate almost as far as they could get from European civilisation, they
have kept on civilising Europe by sheer talent. William Paterson
founded the Bank of England and initiated the National Debt system,
for which you can curse him if you like but I bet you wish you had
done it. Even more astonishing is John Law, the aristocratic prodigy
who was born at the family estate near Edinburgh and pretty well
invented capitalism. It was Law who really worked out the system of
credit, and his ingenious mathematical notions were rejected in
Scotland for the eccentric reason that they seemed likely to increase
the power of government to excess.

Law was not merely a desiccated computer. He fought a duel in
London and killed his man, and had to flee to France where the Duc
d'Orleans became his protector and he became France's first minister
in charge of economic affairs. (He later founded the city of New
Orleans, but this is a trivial by-product of his energy.) If he had
gained even more authority in France, he might have averted the
Revolution, because Law had no patience with the fatuous tax sys-
tem of the country. As it was, he managed to cut the cost of living
for ordinary Frenchman by one-third. He invented paper money.
He founded the Bank of France. He founded the French East India
Company, partly for fun and partly in the hope of ruining England.
He was a noticeable man by anybody's standards.

Cameron and the Adam Brothers and Charles Rennie Mackintosh
put their stamp firmly on European architecture; Adam Smith flung
a half-brick into the stagnant waters of economic science; Walter
Scott invented the historical novel; David Hume transformed
philosophy and woke Kant from his dogmatic slumber, in Kant's
own words. Sir Patrick Geddes invented town-planning. It's a brute
of a job trying to live up to all these meddlers. The poems of Ossian
staggered Europe's consciousness so much that Napoleon always
carried a translation in his knapsack along with his field-marshal's
baton.

It's hard to tell who invented the myth of the dour Scot, because
most of those people were not merely big-domed brains, they were
spellbinders as well. The whole place is a nation of poetic oddities.
There was Daniel Dunglass Home, illegitimate great-uncle of a
British Prime Minister, who established himself as the greatest
spiritualist medium of history. He wandered off to France too, probably because it's difficult to get an audience in a country like Scotland where everybody else is busy putting on a performance of some

Oban : fresh fish

kind simultaneously. The great and the noble fell for him with a crash. Madame de Balzac became his lifelong friend and Dumas was best man at his wedding. The Czar of Russia received him in splendour at Tsarkoe, the palace designed by Cameron. Home transformed the Tuileries into a witches' Sabbat. You couldn't sit down to dinner for massive tables soaring round the room or grand pianos upending themselves, and during one famous performance the Princess Metternich was holding an accordion when, for no reason at all, music poured out of it so sweetly that everybody knew it must be

Fishpacking at Oban

supernatural. They used to bring engineers in to comb the place for wires and mirrors and lumps of illicit electricity, but nobody ever caught him out in a fraud. He materialised a hand that wrote Napoleon's very signature. In later life he was converted to Catholicism, but was soon drummed out of the Vatican accused of sorcery. As he was being ordered out, the table on which an official was writing rose in the air and hung there.

Anybody will tell you that the day of the great characters is past, because people have always said the same thing. At any given moment, you can hardly identify the characters in Scotland for the milling mass of characters who get in the way. Oliver Brown, M.A., whose brains I pick regularly, is one of the legimitate eccentrics himself, and by legitimate eccentric I mean a man who is not interested in being eccentric, but insists on being himself. Oliver is a gentle-spoken and abstemious man of middle age and unobtrusive build who fasts on Christmas Day to demonstrate privately to himself that he is not a Christian. He abominates the scunnersome English yoke foisted on Scotland by that Machiavellian Treaty of Union, but he wouldn't dream of punching anybody to prove his opinion, and one of the reasons why he thinks Scotland is marvellous is that the religious Reformation in this country happened almost without the shedding of blood. An inveterate wearer of the kilt, he isn't bothered at all by the fact that its traditions are dubious; he likes it, and he recently discovered a serious scientific theory that the wearing of trousers may reduce male fertility because of their unnatural restriction of the body.

Most people who have noticed him assume he is a stalwart of the Scottish National Party, but this is the kind of assumption that never works in Scotland, because you no sooner found a nationalist party than another one sets up in opposition, or a dissident group walks out and sets up a rival group. Oliver indeed founded the Scottish Socialist Party, and when I was cheerleading round the I L P stool on May Day demonstrations, I used to see him scattering revolutionary wisdom to his wild-eyed little band of faithful. It looked like a totally unpractical approach to politics, but it was splendid, and I don't know why I should have felt superior, because the I L P was always splitting up too. At that end of the political spectrum, we all believed too fervently in pure principles. Too much to get anywhere as dirty big power groups. We argued the toss and split up and kept right on going. Oliver himself decided that a mass party was a pretty futile way of changing the world, so he left the party he had started himself, and it fell to bits at once. Somebody will now tell me that it is still as lively as ever, but my answer will be that if there is such a thing as a Scottish Socialist Party, it must be a *different* Scottish Socialist Party. In the meantime, Oliver strides onwards on his own, being a Scotsman in his own way and be damned to everybody. He is working on a book about the Auld Alliance, formed between Scotland and France in opposition to England; and he has established that all Scotsmen and all Frenchmen were granted dual nationality officially in the sixteenth century, and that the Scottish end of the bargain wasn't repudiated by the brutal London government until 1906, which means that any Frenchman born in 1905 or earlier is still Scottish, or British, unless we assume that all treaties accepted by monarchist France were automatically nullified in 1789. The whole affair is very conditional, as you can see, but some Scotsman or some Frenchman will arise who will challenge any Government that dares to take his rights away.

The man who has done precisely this kind of thing is Douglas Young, who manages to be an imposing Greek scholar and a poet, philosopher, expert on Scottish language and history and God knows what else. Young is a thin, long arrangement with a superb torn mattress of black beard, and a man of such cultured charm that it is always a pleasure to speak to his waistcoat, which is as high as I can see when we both stand up. In the last war, he elected to decline military service, no doubt for a variety of excellent reasons but primarily to prove that under that same Treaty of Union between Scotland and England, Scotsmen were left free and Scottish and none of them could be obliged to take up arms on orders from Whitehall.

You can't win this kind of fight, of course. Without in any way wishing to impugn the warlike enthusiasm of the Scot, I estimate that if Douglas Young had won his case in a court of law, anything up to a dozen or twenty or more Scots would have asserted their rights by walking out of the British Army. But being Young, he took on the legal system single-handed and conducted his own case at immense length and with delicious eloquence and cogency; at the end of which he was thrown out of court and into jail regardless. He went under protest, but cheerfully and politely as always.

We laugh a lot in Scotland at the genuinely passionate Nationalists, because we're as apathetic as most people, but some of them are

Jack Munro,
a medical student

taken very seriously in high quarters. Wee Rab Wilkie, who looks
like a mildly tortured saint with a wildcat slumbering somewhere far
beneath, isn't actually under twenty-four-hour surveillance by M I 5
as he often claims with a delighted giggle in his romantic moods, but
the security boys have closed in on him now and then at airports and
such-like places in case he was slipping off to rally a revolting army
to seize the G.P.O. At this possibility, his friends burst into giggles,
though the ruthless freedom fighter is lurking about in him somewhere. If he ever found himself at the head of a revolutionary army,
everybody would end up talking the night away – under meticulous
chairmanship, it's true, and none would talk in more elegant gem-
like prose than Rab until he leaned back against a convenient wall,
smiled and fell quietly asleep as a gentleman should.

These three contemporaries have very little in common except
that they are all dominies (maybe there's something about teaching
that makes a man value independence) and they will all go any
lengths for their suffering motherland, or fatherland. But you can
scratch nearly any wide-awake Scotsman and find a nationalist.

George Macleod ought to know better, being a minister of religion and everything, but you can't spend much time with him before you get a whiff of the old fervour. An aristocrat by birth (not that that means anything whatever in Scotland) and a Socialist by conviction, Macleod is another big Scotsman, with strong bones and a tough kindly face who would probably have made a formidable actor or many other things if he hadn't been cursed with principles, and is rather suspicious of his own natural oratorical powers. He managed to divert a lot of his nationalist enthusiasm into rebuilding Iona, with his own hands and the volunteers he infected.

We also have Jack House, the most tireless writer and talker in Scottish journalism, and a dangerously formidable citizen because he has never been seen to lose his temper even while he was slashing holes in pompous people or institutions. House demonstrated the superiority of Scottish elementary education by being the champion of that old encyclopaedia game the Round-Britain Quiz in the days of paraffin radio, and when he suddenly became a Liberal Parliamentary candidate, a lot of people thought it must be a joke because he cracks jokes all the time. An English newspaper dismissed him as a lightweight, but he always carries plenty of weight where he wants to. He was once accosted in a pub by a man with a dense Glasgow accent who accused him of rolling his r's artificially on the radio because he sounded so terrible Scotch. But when a Scotsman is up to something serious, he *is*. He's terrible Scotch. And bystanders are well advised to stand aside. Horo, the noo, Gregalach, and so on.

THE HARD STUFF

Whisky is interesting not primarily because it's an intoxicating beverage, but because it's a mystery. They make it in factories all right, the same as people make plastic cheese and homogenized asbestos boiling fowls, but the element of natural chance is still strong in Scotch whisky. It can't be made anywhere else, and it can't be made identical even in any two places in Scotland.

To describe it as crudely as possible, Scotch whisky is a distillation of beer. Barley grains are encouraged to germinate, gently warmed and infused with the smoke from burning peat. This process produces malt, which is milled fine and put in water, and the liquor is fermented by the addition of yeast. The resultant brew is enclosed in a still, and gentle heat boils away the alcohol and leaves the rest, since alcohol boils at a lower temperature than water. The alcohol vapour goes up into a long thin tube where it cools back to liquid, and that liquid is whisky.

The same process, roughly, applies to gin or vodka or methylated spirits. What distinguishes whisky is the curious nature of Scotland itself.

The peat is vital, and fairly large areas of Scotland are composed of peat, which is a sunken layer of decomposed vegetation of the same nature as coal, but so much younger that it is still spongy and friable. As a fuel, it is nowhere near coal, but its smoke has a dense woody fragrance which is one of the odd components of Scotch. Another essential is the nature of Scottish water, especially Highland water taken from the stream. It sounds absurd, but water running down from the mountains runs over soil so infinitely variable that two burns only yards apart will produce two quite distinct whiskies. You first find a stream, and then build a distillery.

In addition to that, the distilling of Scotch remains an art even now that it is done on a huge scale with high-class scientific equipment. When it is first distilled, the alcohol that comes out is violent, crude and impure as any illicit poteen, and it is distilled again; and this time the early fumes are led away to be discarded, likewise the last fumes, and only the stuff boiled off during the middle of the run are taken. The decision as to when to turn the tap on and off rests with a man, a human being, and not a spectroscope or an electronic litmus paper. The making of whisky remains a knacky human affair, acquired by experience and instinct.

The other alarming thing is that the same still, using the same burn-water, will never produce precisely the same whisky. This didn't matter in the days when the stuff was made in the kitchen and whatever came out was good enough to keep the cold out. Now that whisky is big business with brand names and an export trade, the blender has to bring in all kinds of whiskies to add to the distillery's own liquor so that the same flavour is blended year after year. He does this with his nose, whose memory never fails.

For these and other reasons, Scotch whisky is the safest and purest hard liquor made in the world, but I have to add that alcohol is not really good for people at all, being a drug that can fuddle the mind and lower resistance to death by freezing, and in some people, produce addiction, madness and death. I have to say this because it's true, and because no Scotsman has a simple attitude to the drink. The phenomenon of whisky demonstrates better than anything else the ambiguous nature of old Scotia.

Some other peoples, for all I know, may look on drink with mild distaste or mild affection. In Scotland we have to love it with besotted passion or detest it as the instrument of the devil; or more usually, both at once.

At one extreme, you will find the soak who has recognised his master in the bottle and is slugging his way to hell. At the other, the stern teetotaller who rejects it and is preaching himself to somewhere. In the middle, you will find the rest of us, mixed up to hell. We know it's good and we know it's bad and we're liable to deliver temperance sermons as soon as the fumes from the third glass have reached our cerebral cortex.

We enjoy a magnificent hypocrisy in our attitude to booze. When

I first asked my grocer to include a bottle in the weekly order, he smiled knowingly and said,

'A small suggestion of something under the potatoes?'

That was the old code signal of the Glasgow church-going classes when they wanted a nip smuggled into the house without its being seen by the neighbours or even mentioned between the contracting parties. In Shettleston, on the old road out from Glasgow to Edinburgh, there's a pub set back three feet from the adjacent buildings, and I swear it was built like that so that church elders could walk along close to the wall and then disappear by magic. When the national president of some federation arrived in Inverness on a Sunday night to address the local branch on the Monday, the branch secretary escorted him to the Station Hotel and asked him if he would mind going in by the side door because it would never do for the President to be seen entering licensed premises on the Sabbath. (Talking about the Sabbath, there is a much older story of an acquiescent Highland chambermaid who flounced out of a guest's room in horror because, she said, she would never bring herself to fornicate with a man who whistled on a Sunday. But it may not be a true story.)

Until 1963, the insane whisky-lust of the Scots was curbed, in theory, by the famous Bona Fide Traveller law of glassy-eyed memory. This law attempted to combine national abstention with local indulgence, and the principle was that people could not be served with intoxicants on the Sabbath, except that footsore travellers would be allowed refreshment on their route. In practice, this meant that if you lived in a village like Gartocharn on Loch Lomondside, where there is a pleasantly warm little hotel, you could go to the door and be turned brutally away; but a friend driving out from Glasgow to have tea with you was legally entitled to go in and get sloshed.

There was always a lot of theoretical argument about what constituted a bona fide traveller within the meaning of the Act. Some people said it was a man who had journeyed at least 15 miles; some 7; some 3. In fact it was never clearly established. But the squalid Scottish topers discovered the obvious loophole immediately. They could evacuate Village A and get a noggin in Village B, while the population of Village B were back at A ordering rounds. It was a black day for the local bus hirers when the bona fide law was abandoned. Halfway between the remote villages of Balmacara and Kyle of Lochalsh, on the beautiful lonely road among the immemorial hills, there stood a notice painted on both sides with the legend 'Remember the Sabbath day, to keep it holy' so that it could be read by the topers of each village as they walked towards and past one another on their way to a legitimate bar counter.

A BBC producer, a man of liberal appetites, found himself suffering as the house guest of a staunch churchgoer in Argyllshire, the president of the local Temperance Association and a man of rigorous and endless principle. After a gloomy supper presaging an endless night, the host invited the guest to inspect the garden, which was invisible in the winter night. At the bottom of the garden was a heap of rubbish from which the good man drew out two earth-encrusted bottles of the real stuff and passed one over to be drunk there and then, neat, in the forgiving dark.

We can do that with a clear conscience, because the devious Scot, more than most people, tends to favour the Doctrine of Election, which is to say that it is our duty to condemn sin in the name of God, but each one of us, and nobody else, has a private arrangement with the Almighty whereby our own misdemeanours will be recognised as harmless and nobody's business. We are the Elect.

The most terrifying description of this good Scottish neurosis to be written in modern times is contained in John Buchan's superb

The "Maid of the loch" at Balloch Pier

novel *Witch Wood*. The most famous of all time is Robert Burns'
hilarious poem 'Holy Willie's Prayer', in which a good upright man
addresses himself privately to the Lord with a progress report and a
request for action. He says, among other things:

> Yet I am here, a chosen sample,
> To show Thy grace is great and ample:
> I'm here a pillar o' Thy temple
>   Strong as a rock,
> A guide, a buckler and example
>   Tae a' Thy flock!
>
> But yet, O Lord! confess I must:
> At times I'm fash'd wi' fleshly lust;
> An' sometimes, too, in warldly trust,
>   Vile self gets in;
> But Thou remembers we are dust,
>   Defiled wi' sin.
>
> O Lord! yestreen, Thou kens, wi' Meg –
> Thy pardon I sincerely beg –
> O, may't ne'er be a living plague
>   To my dishonour!
> An' I'll ne'er lift a lawless leg
>   Again upon her.
>
> Lord, bless Thy chosen in this place,
> For here Thou has a chosen race!
> But God confound their stubborn face,
>   An' blast their name,
> Wha bring Thy elders to disgrace
>   An' open shame!
>
> Lord, mind Gau'n Hamilton's deserts
> He drinks, an' swears, an' plays at cartes,
> Yet has sae monie takin arts
>   Wi' great and sma',
> Frae God's ain Priest the people's hearts
>   He steals awa.

And when we chasten'd them therefore,
Thou kens how he bred sic a splore
And set the warld in a roar
   O' laughin at us:
Curse Thou his basket and his store,
   Kail an' potatoes!

But, Lord, remember me and mine
Wi' mercies temporal and divine,
That I for grace an' gear may shine
   Excell'd by nane;
And a' the glory shall be Thine –
   Amen, Amen!

Burns was brought hard up against the rugged tradition of Scottish hypocrisy, but he couldn't have demolished it so finely, or enjoyed it so much, if he hadn't been a Scot with the embryo of it that

Burns Cottage, Ayr

he recognised in himself. We all have it, crafty old Jekylls and Hydes that we are. The craftiest of us, like Burns, form secret societies so that we can sternly walk past the pub door and get tanked up privately in the club – just as Burns formed the Bachelors, where he could be wild and discreet simultaneously. It was in a curious club that I first heard Holy Willie's Prayer from the lips of Charlie Brookes, who is the greatest living reciter of the Scottish poet's works.

Charlie, to digress for a moment, is a retired schoolmaster with a piercing eye and a tiny white goatee, and a disconcerting fashion of changing the subject or laughing abruptly at some private revelation of the wonder of life. His arms tend to fly out from his body at inconvenient moments when he's wound up, but always gracefully, as long as you've moved your drink out of danger. He is one of the ornaments of a slightly Burnsian association by the name of 'Ours', a bizarre conspiracy whose records date back to 1871 and which is therefore the oldest literary society in Scotland.

'Ours' itself is a mixture of Burns and Dickens. Membership cannot be sought or bought, but occurs only by mysterious invitation. It meets in a small single clubroom whose walls are festooned with cartoons and manuscripts ancient and modern, and the furniture is mainly a big table and a lot of old chairs, one of them actually a Robert Burns relic. While other clubs have lived and died in hundreds, Ours survives and holds fast to obsolete ritual.

Every Friday evening through each winter, the members meet and sit round the table, and one of them is formally introduced as the essayist, with a flower in his buttonhole for the occasion. This grim duty falls on every member once a year, and having delivered a thoughtful paper on literature or philosophy or whatever he first thought of, he then sits down while every member present is called upon to criticise him. The criticisms may occasionally be kindly, but the tradition calls for savagery.

The reason for the unusual name of this society stems from a nineteenth century meeting of the club, which was originally entitled the Glasgow Literary and Philological Society. The chairman of the evening, in proposing the toast of the Society at the end, found that his tongue repeatedly flopped out of the side of his mouth on the second word, and in desperation finally said, 'You know wharra mean, Ours.'

The reason why there are so many Scotch jokes about drink is

precisely the reason that there are so many about religion and sex –
you joke about a subject only when it inspires you with both respect
and guilt. The same thing applies to money, to which our attitude is
similar.

A man went into a pub in Wishaw and had a quiet word with the
barman, who knew him as a regular customer. There was a problem
to be discussed, because the customer's brother had just come out of
a mental home and would probably be in later that evening.

'He's absolutely all right,' the customer explained, 'no ugly
tricks or anything. The only thing . . . you know, kind of daft . . . is
that he thinks the tinfoil caps off milk-bottles are *money*. But if I'm

not here, just serve him anything he likes and count it up, and I'll square up tomorrow.'

On the next day the customer came back. The barman reported that the brother had indeed been in, and had run up a bill of seven pounds.

'Seven pounds!'

'Well, he's a very nice chap, stood drinks for everybody. I've got all the milk-bottle tops here, I'm not trying to cheat you.'

'No, no, I know you wouldn't cheat me,' said the customer. 'As long as Wullie had a good time that's fine. Seven pounds, eh? Well now, have you got change of a dustbin lid?'

Holidaymakers at Oban

HUMAN FLESH

The road down by the Ayrshire coast is one of the showpieces of stern old Caledonia because this is Caledonia without the sternness. There's a big four-lane highway from Glasgow to Kilmarnock that infects drivers with madness of the heart, and nobody notices the sinister bleakness of the Fenwick Moor because it's only a picture that somebody's unrolling past the side windows; and after that you're in the lush rich farmland where the brown soil smells of money. Maybe this is all an illusion, since this is the landscape where Robert Burns' old man had such a rotten time trying to beat a living out of the earth. Anyway, it's a very imposing piece of real estate in which many strange things have happened.

There's the little village of Stewarton, which is quite easy to miss altogether, and which is notable for being the home of Eric Clarke the cartoonist, who spent twenty years trying to prevent me from buying a Bentley. He was on his thirty-third car then. He had started off with a Morris two-seater and every one after that got smaller and smaller. He was mad on small cars, and furious with contempt at the idea of a lousy columnist owning a useless big gas-guzzler, and if he had been able to go on the way he was, he would have ended up driving a sewing-machine. It was war to the hilt on the petrol companies, and his greatest triumph in recollection was an absurd little whirring machine made in Germany with only two cylinders. He fixed that. He took out one of the plugs and said it ran even better on only one. Then he would change it for something even smaller and rip off the body to make it more economical, and build a tiny tin shed on top of what was left. When we worked together on *The Daily*

Record he ruled my ambitions like a demented Macduff and kept reporting that he had found a 50 c.c. invalid chair that would go as fast as I would ever be able to drive.

It was under Clarke's sneering guidance that I devised my celebrated Plonk system of personal transport, which I have preached on street corners and in philosophical associations with no response whatever except guffaws from the yahoos. He got at me so insidiously that I even went off pushbikes because they take up too much road. The Plonk is a transparent plastic bag, held rigid by internal air pressure, and inside it a man rests upright on a bicycle saddle on top of a bit of broom handle. At the foot of the broom handle is a minute engine driving a heavy iron wheel, and this maintains the vehicle in the erect position by gyroscopic force. The wheel has a groove round the rim, like a pulley, and the whole contraption sits on the telephone wires so that we can do away with roads altogether. The Plonk is the only idea I've ever had that Clarke can look at without snarling, and don't think I'm not grateful.

His constant message to me was Economy and Efficiency, and it got so that I was frightened to open my mouth at all in case it reminded him of a venturi tube. When he was working as a staff cartoonist, he was the senior of a small band of aborigines who used to share a studio on the fourth floor, where nobody would ever find them, and sometimes for weeks on end they would devise convenient weapons with bits of wood and elastic, with which they could endlessly enact the battle of Powder River, or Solway Moss, or whatever Eric had been reading in his comic that month. Some of their constructions were quite complicated, firing things like small aeroplanes or ping-pong balls, and all four of them would often spend two whole days crouching under their desks waving white flags and gibbering.

The most serious-minded of the four, Bill McLachlan, eventually acquired a kind of home-made shell-shock at the sight of anything that might be a disguised fire-arm, and passed an entire morning trying to pluck up courage to get into the studio to work in face of a pasteboard tube which Clarke wedged in the letterbox and abandoned. In fact, he emigrated to Canada after this and was never heard of again. But at least he won't be afraid of grizzly bears. Another of the quartette was Ramsay, who drew the pictures in this book but who has fled to the cringing safety of London, the yellow dog.

The Market, Inverness

Eric was always up to something, and he still is. Other people might talk vaguely about buying a couple of tropical fish one day. With Clarke, it was that very day and no other. As soon as tropical fish occurred to him, he converted his entire house into an aquarium, or at least the bits of it that weren't already a car conversion factory. I always got the impression that if he had a vague notion in the middle of the night, he would leap from bed and instantly start sawing and hammering to make it real. Things always seemed to be *happening* in Stewarton, bangs in the night, mistaken identities, houses flying away. It is a quiet, pleasant little place. I finally discovered this because Eric took me there, to supervise my possession of the car which he had finally allowed me to buy. It was a tiny thing, and it went like a rocket when he drove me home in it and parked it outside my door. He had a way of making cars work. As soon as he left, the car stopped dead and never moved again until I had it taken to pieces and rebuilt. It knew I wasn't Eric Clarke. If the Martians ever land at Stewarton and the sky is filled with odd blue lights and whining noises, people will stir irritably in their beds and then somebody will say, 'It must be Eric again.' And everybody will go back to sleep.

Other people, who see Stewart merely as the name on a signpost, accelerate down and flash past in case they hear strange music and get lured away forever, or even worse, involved in something Clarke had just thought of that very minute. He himself once lived out a genuine Lord Dunsany short story in a dark Ayrshire farmhouse, with Charlie Stewart the comedy dancer, who was brought up in the same district. Everybody else had gone to bed, and the old friends sat there talking about old times until the cheerful fire sank to a dim glow and the words died away into a comfortable silence. I know this sounds like the old *Strand Magazine*, but it's the way it happened. There was silence for perhaps ten minutes, and Clarke wondered idly if his companion had fallen asleep.

He glanced at the other chair and saw Stewart's eye glinting in the firelight. Feeling, irrationally, that he had been caught out, Clarke made a meaningless grimace, and Stewart, falling at once into his friend's mood, twisted his own features in response. The two men continued to regard each other in silence. Feeling that something further was expected of him, Clarke pulled a grotesque face, and after an interval, Stewart replied with an insane contortion.

Still in total silence, the two men found themselves in the grip of a lunatic contest; their grimaces grew wilder and more painful, until a horrid suspicion began to burgeon in Clarke's honest mind: that the contest which had begun for him as a foolish childish game had by chance or coincidence stimulated an actual dormant insanity in his friend. For Stewart's eyes were now bulging in unmistakable terror even as his lips twisted in a maniac leer. And suddenly Stewart jerked out of his chair and cried, 'Are you all right, Eric?' in the same instant that Clarke was reaching out a hand and gasping 'Are you all right, Charlie?'

'I thought you had gone loony,' said both men simultaneously.

They sat back trembling and avoided each other's eyes. That's the story they told me, anyway. Personally, I've always suspected that they *had* gone mad.

But frightening things are always happening in Ayrshire. William Murdoch, the man who invented gas lighting, was born in Lugar in this county, and he has always frightened me. When Scotland got too small for him, he walked all the way to Birmingham to look for a job, and he got it because Matthew Boulton the steam-engine tycoon fell in love with Murdoch's hat. It was a delicate lump of millinery which Murdoch had fashioned from a solid block of wood on his own lathe.

They have a thing every year at Irvine called the Marymass Fair, and it's the first place where I ever saw tartan horses. I was an earnest young columnist at the time, and I thought I was some pumpkin, I can tell you. I used to sit in tramcars reading my own column and hooting, so that people would look over my shoulder and I could confess modestly that I was the big name on page two. They had a lot of trouble with me before they abolished the Glasgow trams. Anyway, this has nothing to do with the story. I went down to the Marymass Fair because I was always a hog for wee folklory stories about the leedle seemple people who cling to the ancient ways of their ancestors. I could vomit when I think of myself. Nevertheless, I arrived in Irvine on a Saturday morning, with my fair young bride, because she was sick of being left at home while I went off boozing on expenses, and we got soaked to the skin as we bolted from the bus to a shop door and spent a merry half-hour dripping and reading the comic postcards.

It rained all day, and we inched from doorway to doorway, loathing the seemple leedle people who were sitting in their kitchens with their feet in the fireplace. But pretty soon the procession started,

Houseboats at Balloch, Loch Lomond

because rain has never stopped anything in Ayrshire. It was a string of horse-drawn floats, and an unusual number of Irvine horses in those days were white. They were dressed to kill, with green and red cockades all over them, and what with the rain and the cheap dyes, by the time they reached us there were three complete horses who had turned tartan. Hard-faced farmers in pub doorways were crossing themselves or touching their rabbits' feet, if they had rabbits with them, and muttering old Ayrshire prophecies like

'When orra horses jine a clan
Drink up and ha'e anither wan.'

So we drank up, and fell in with a fast-talking man from Bridgeton called Jimmy Broon, who made no secret of the fact that he was a bookie. It's odd how bookies turn up everywhere. He was travelling with his son and a leather bag and a pair of very light-soled shoes, and I knew from the way he kept plying us with liquor that he had an eye on the fair young bride, because he kept stumbling against her in a very complimentary way. I was proud rather than huffed at this show of casual lust, and after some witty conversation it was agreed that Jimmy's son and I should venture out like brave idiots to the race-track, in case there was anything doing, while Jimmy and my tender young wife stayed cravenly indoors.

It wasn't an Ascot-type race-track, but more of an accidental

Fishermen : Portree, Skye

moon landscape near the beach, where the horses raced round a fairly flat area round the base of a small hill; and the big attraction was that the race was for cart-horses only. The rain never stopped for a second. A great mob of the cart-horses were mounted by their carters and stood about steaming till nobody could stand it any longer, and then somebody shouted off and they were off. I was glad I had come. Fine-drawn Arab bloodstock is all very well, but you haven't seen anything till you've seen Clydesdales as big as bunga-lows at full pelt. From where we were standing, the damp seascape was entirely hidden by a line of massive rumps, and then the whole shebang disappeared round the other side of the hill.

Nothing happened for some seconds, and then I realised that the sea was *jerking*. Or I was jerking. A heavy seismic rhythm had started to vibrate the Ayrshire coast and the sky thundered. My teeth were clanging in my jaw when a cloud of steam appeared round the other end of the hill, and through it there came the flaring nostrils and glaring eyes of an eruption of Clydesdales, with dwarfed tiny men hovering above them. I would have run for my life if the earth hadn't been heaving under me. They came down the home straight in a wall of sweat, divots the size of armchairs flew from their hooves and left spoor that could have buried collie dogs, or earnest young columnists. I was still twitching when I got back to Irvine, and I kept spilling things and biting my tongue.

Meanwhile, back at the pub, Jimmy had organised a Lucullan feast of sausages to demonstrate the solidarity of the working class, and he was in the middle of a perfectly convincing story of how he had once made a train journey back from a race meeting crouched outside on the running board, listening to the passengers inside discuss who would get the first kick at him if they ever caught him.

'I'm the only guy that ever conned Billy Butlin,' he stated calmly. 'You mind he ran the big fairground at the Empire Exhibition. Well. Hard times, you know? I was, eh, temporarily absent, from the bookie game, tell you the truth I was workin' under an alias at the time, waitin' for the heat to go aff. So, eh, I moseys along for a bit of reconnaissance, so this buildin' foreman says, Hey, we're stuck for nails, could you go up to the store and get some?'

'Oh, very keen, touch the cap, honest British workman, that was me,' Jimmy recalled in admiration. 'Off to the store for the nails. I might have been anybody, the place was burstin' wi' people, but the storeman was the untrustful type. *But.* While I was telling him to kindly supply the nails, my man, we can't waste valuable time chewing the fat, who turns up but Mr Butlin hisself. Very impressed with James's enthusiasm – Billy knew a human dynamo when he seen one, so he tells the storeman to supply this worker with anything he wanted and keep the wheels humming. Nails? Jesus, before I was done I was drawin' absolute forests out that store an' selling them to the contractor up the street.'

The reason why I remember Jimmy, apart from his ungrudging admiration for my taste in wives, is that I have always believed an honest resourceful Scotsman will always come out on top. And this brings me naturally to the notable achievements of Sawney Beane, one of the least appreciated of Scotsmen, who operated an industrial project farther south in Ayrshire which has never been equalled for sheer dash and single-mindedness.

I had better say at once that like many Scots before him, including Bruce and Kenneth McAlpin and that lot, Sawney Beane has probably been exaggerated. The best historian in the field, William Roughead, has regretfully decided that the whole Beane saga may be no more than legend, in fact, but it is so adorned with circumstance and local colour that it must be told and it's hard not to believe.

Mr Beane was born about eight miles from Edinburgh on an unrecorded date in the sixteenth century, of honest and laborious parents, but honest labour made him ill, and he ran away in his youth to seek better things. Naturally, he fell into the company of a vicious woman, because there was a lot of them around in old Scotland. The couple enjoyed their viciousness, however, and wandered the country until they found a commodious cave near Bennane Head in Ayrshire, and there they set up in business. Soon they had founded a community so self-sufficient that for twenty-five years, neither ever had to go near a town or village.

But although nobody ever saw Mr or Mrs Beane, the district began to acquire an unfortunate reputation. People began to disappear, and other people began to talk.

The word murder was freely bandied about, and 'abundance of innocent travellers and inn-keepers were executed, on suspicion of being the murderers, yet all was in vain.'

The Ayrshire population figures were suffering badly, since half the people on the roads were vanishing and the other half were being hanged all the time. So many inn-keepers were being hanged that many others abandoned their inns and emigrated to find safer jobs. This in turn produced a shortage of inns, and forced travellers to make longer journeys, and disappear faster. In the end, the magistrates got tired of executing folk without effect, and trusted wholly to Providence for the solution of the crisis.

Providence turned up in the persons of a man and wife, travellers sharing one horse, who were ambushed on the road near Bennane Head by a resolute band of monsters. As the raiders closed in, the wife fell off the horse. Several of the attackers leapt on her and murdered her instantly, cut her throat, and proceeded to drink her blood. While they were busy, the husband laid about with his sword, and by a lucky accident, there appeared a party of twenty-five rustics who had been visiting a fair. The criminals took flight and fled, and the hysterical husband was able to show the other travellers the

On the Caledonian Canal,
near Inverness

mangled remains of his wife, which were gathered up and taken to the magistrates in Glasgow.

The business was too big for mere magistrates, and the King himself was informed; James VI, that is, the Wisest Fool in Christendom. He was the one who hated tobacco and didn't go much on women either, but he was even more down on murder, and set out personally from Edinburgh at the head of four hundred men to clean up Ayrshire. Even the four hundred would never have found the Beanes if they hadn't brought dogs, which kept barking at a small hole in the rocks till the searchers were forced to investigate more closely. They found that the little hole was the entrance to a commodious cave packed with Beanes.

But worse than the Beanes, who now numbered forty-six, were the other things in the cave. Limbs, arms, thighs and feet of men, women and children were hung up in rows, like dried beef. A great many limbs lay in pickle, and heaps of coin, jewellery, pistols, clothes were scattered round the cave. This was no ordinary murder case.

During their twenty-five years' tenancy of the cave, Mr and Mrs

Beane had begat children, grandchildren and other confused relations. The count at this point was eight sons, six daughters, eighteen grandsons, fourteen grand-daughters. They had lived by murdering something over a thousand travellers and eating them. Apart from the current stock displayed in the cave, various bones were found buried under the beach nearby. The horrified Royal party, having loaded themselves with spoil, escorted the tribe to Edinburgh.

No trial was necessary, under an ancient Scottish law relating to murderers caught red-handed. A jamboree was organised, at which the males of the tribe had various parts of their bodies removed and burned before their eyes, after which their hands and legs were severed and they were allowed to bleed to death. The females, after spectating at this ceremony, were arranged in three heaps and burned to death. To the disgust of the witnesses, they all died without a trace of repentance, screaming the most objectionable oaths all the time. Cannibalism, however, has never really caught on in Scotland since.

DISGRACE
IN THE FAMILY

Paisley has an abbey and a lot of skyscraper flats and an eccentric boulder, and that is not my derisive description, that's what the thing is called officially. It stands in a little yard on the main street, and it's eccentric because according to the glacial history of the district, it has no right to be there at all. Paisley has the highest ratio of amateur poets to population of any place in Scotland, and stands on the River Cart about twelve miles from Glasgow, which somewhat overshadows it as an individual town. Politicians of olden times used to advise one another to keep their eyes on Paisley. The town is also the home of the great thread mills of the Coats family, which stands high in the old industrial aristocracy of the country. Coats' mills occur briefly in one of the best true melodramatic tales I ever heard, from a Paisley man who was there at the time, and I am changing his name merely because the story *is* true, and a lot of people know him, and the main characters are still alive.

Sanny, as I shall describe him, was a small boy with many uncles and aunts, all in the thread-mill stratum of Paisley. Most of his relatives worked in the mills or were married to mill-workers or lived in the mill orbit. They were the mills of God, you might have said. Now when you get an industry as big as that, you'll always get minor irregularities, and from time to time the management worried about the number of bobbins that disappeared without trace. The little wooden bobbins were worth a fraction of a penny, and workers would take a couple home for the wife, or the children, without any sensation of guilt, everybody could understand that; but theft is

Luss Church, Loch Lomond

theft, and can't be formally condoned, and from time to time the management would act fierce about it.

One day they decided to put the screw on, and to make it as simple as possible, one worker out of the thousands going out through the gates was stopped and searched. Like many others, he had a couple of bobbins in his jacket pocket. He was Sanny's Uncle Dave.

'You've got to understand, of course,' Sanny warned me when he recalled the story, 'that we were a very respectable family. Chronic respectability. Everybody else would half-inch a bobbin or two and that was okay, but getting caught isn't respectable. But that wasn't the worst. The company decided to make a proper example of Uncle Dave and call in the police. The police! In our family! It's all right laughing, but in the nineteen-twenties, the only thing anybody owned was a respectable reputation. Everybody the whole tribe, was knocked sideways. My Uncle Dave got a summons to the Burgh Court and they fined him two pounds.

'Of course, nobody told me what was going on because I was only the wean. But they had a family conference, honest to God, a complete family conference, and what gets me is that it was one of my aunties – by marriage, that is; she wasn't even *in* the family – it was her that kept insisting that the family could never hold its head up again as long as Uncle Dave was there to be pointed at. Aye, I know this is ridiculous, but my God, before they were finished, she had it fixed up that he would be shipped off to the Colonies! For a two-quid fine! You don't know what respectability means if you've never met this auntie of mine. They had a whip-round for a boat ticket to Canada, and Uncle Dave just took it. He didn't have the strength to fight back, he knew he was guilty.

'No, you'll never believe this, but Auntie Thingmy had him shut out of his own home as well. It was four days to the sailing, and he had to vanish that very minute. My own father was the only one that would take him in. I was only a kid, I thought it was fine having Uncle Dave staying with us, but I knew there was something up. On the last morning, before he left, he was sitting at breakfast and all of a sudden he burst into tears. It was horrible. I had never heard of a grown man crying, especially a man like Uncle Dave – I know now he was only a youngster at the time, of course, but he was a big adult man to me. I couldn't believe it. The old man tried to cheer him up and then I was sent to school. By the time I got back, Uncle Dave was away and I never saw him again.'

Thus honour was satisfied according to one old Scottish code, the code of visible righteousness before God and man. But the reason why this is my favourite Paisley story is that it had another chapter, still firmly in the melodrama tradition.

Decades went by. The shame of Uncle Dave was covered over by time, and only the vaguest stories drifted back from Canada about his continued existence. The war came and went. And the very same Auntie, Auntie Marjorie, decided to visit Canada to see relatives of her own – everybody in Scotland has relatives in Canada. Visiting Canada just after the war was a good game, because it was forbidden to carry any money across the Atlantic from Britain, and all hospitality had to be provided free by the lucky Canadian relations. Auntie Marjorie went and had a fine time. Before she left for home, it came to her in distant memory that the town she was visiting might be the town where Uncle Dave had last been heard of. She wasn't surprised that she couldn't find his name in the telephone book, because a man so shiftless wasn't likely to own a telephone; but a sense of duty weighed on her, because after all this long time she felt that Dave should be forgiven, and have the comfort of knowing it, and it was up to her to make an effort to deliver this message of mercy. She asked in a local store if anybody had ever heard of a McMurdo, and the manager looked doubtful and said there was only one McMurdo he knew of, in the house beyond the crossing a mile

A final check at the distillery

out of town. A big house, he said, and Auntie Marjorie was doubtful too, but always a woman of resolute principle, she walked out of town and found the big house, and walked up half-a-mile of drive-way to the front door and rang the bell. And the delicious thing about this incident is that Auntie Marjorie herself described it, as proof that she had always been right about Uncle Dave.

A servant came to the door, and Auntie explained that she had come from Scotland looking for a relative who had left Paisley over twenty years ago, and that he might just possibly be the same David McMurdo. The servant agreed that this was possible, and asked her to wait in the hall. The look of the hall cheered her up, because it was stinking with money and it's more fun forgiving a rich man than a deadbeat. After ten minutes the servant returned and said that she had found the right Mr McMurdo, but that Mr McMurdo was busy and couldn't see her.

A Glasgow news vendor

AULD REEKIE

There are two distinct and conflicting strains in the Scottish character: the devil-may-care ancient Celtic lust which is always shouting
'To hell wi' poverty, heave another pea in the soup!' and the stern
ancient Celtic righteousness which is simultaneously turning the gas
off under the pot in case anybody gets a free heat. Now that I've said
that, I realise at once that you could say the same thing about the
character of any people anywhere, but it's the kind of thing we
always say about the Scottish character, to keep us cheery, and we
reckon we have established a monopoly of the schizophrenia market.
    Edinburgh is like that, stern and grey and gruesomely respectable
and seething a bit with drink and dark desires and hot flesh, for all I
know, behind its historied dark stones. I thought it was a scream the
first time I saw it, because I had hitch-hiked all the way from Glasgow at the age of eleven only to discover that Edinburgh had
chocolate-coloured tramcars, and everybody knew that tramcars
were supposed to be green and yellow.
    Some time later I realised that Edinburgh had additional charms,
because to the Capital city Glaswegians were as anonymous as Man-
cunians or Manchurians. That forty-mile train ride took you into a
foreign country, and slavering young sensualists, who would never
have had the gall to con a hotel clerk in Glasgow, could stride into
Edinburgh as man and wife without causing a twitch because, as an
Edinburgh man told me later, all Glaswegians look alike.
    Glasgow folk like to think of Edinburgh as beautiful but cold,
and the difference according to Jack House is that in Edinburgh,
breeding is considered good form, whereas in Glasgow it's con-

sidered good fun. There is also a legend about a Glasgow football
club which held a raffle. The first prize was a week's holiday in
Edinburgh and the second prize was a fortnight's holiday in Edinburgh. This is all right as a gag, but Edinburgh is a great place to
visit, and every visit will bring its own delights and surprises. The
tourist attractions, in order of priority, are Rose Street, the Festival,
the Castle and Holyrood. Rose Street is remembered with shudders
of pleasure by the cognoscenti all over the world because this narrow
thoroughfare, running obscurely parallel to Princes Street, appears
to be composed wholly of pubs, ranging all the way from tacketty-
boot, spit-in-the-sawdust howffs to elegant lounges and literary
hangouts. Gay young blades sometimes accept it as a chapter in their
education to take drink in every single one, and they can have it. The
literary one is the Abbotsford, where you can't throw a pint measure
without stunning two poets, or at least one painter and three people
from the BBC. The food and drink are good, and to avoid mis-
understandings, I may add that it is not necessary to throw the pint

measure. A well-timed remark in Cantonese or Sanskrit is less of a strain.

Before I realised the precise tone of the place, I once sat down beside Tyrone Guthrie in this very bar and addressed him familiarly because I thought he was simply a bloke. He was very nice about it. At various times you could also jostle elbows with most of the literary figures of Scotland, and if you can't always do that now, the reason presumably is that back in the old days, nobody had twigged yet that they *were* literary figures. Be careful in case the routine bar-fly without a name is going to be reassessed as a giant in twenty years. I think, though I don't know, that Compton Mackenzie probably presided over the conversaziones at one time. If he didn't, he should have, as an Edinburgh institution.

Mackenzie was in fact born in West Hartlepool, so as to be near his mother, who was there at the time. His hereditary claims to Scottishness are about as tenuous as my own, but he made the grade all right by adoption, which is more logical than birth. Since he had fairly well retired from pub society by the time I met him, he was a tough man to get to at all. His second wife, who I am sorry to say has since died, was a zealously motherly lady who worked unceasingly to keep pests away, and she had plenty. As a converted Catholic, Mackenzie could never resist a sob story from a broke Irishman, and they beat a ravine to his door. It took me ten days of negotiation to get to see the man, and then only for half-an-hour, but the half-hour stretched until I had to be loaded into a taxi and poured down the street.

If I can be cheeky enough to make an assessment of Compton Mackenzie, I will have to be even cheekier and say that his jolly romp novels about Ben Nevis strike me as only very mildly funny, but I must say that if the public makes a mad rush for them, good luck to him. It's wonderful to see an author making money. The *Four Winds of Love* bowled me clean over when I was eighteen and it still has the stuff in it. What always delighted me in Mackenzie was his hard moral sense and his shining style as a writer of logic. I wish I had been in court when he was tried under the Official Secrets Act after the first war and ran rings round the Admiralty. Some of his best sentences occur in his recent book *On Moral Courage*, and in his annotations to *Walls Have Mouths*, in which he takes law and judges meticulously to pieces before your very eyes.

It was fiendishly cunning of me to have read *Walls Have Mouths*,

Charlotte Square, Edinburgh

because when I finally was ushered into the Mackenzie den, that's what got me in. In a moment he had pressed a hospitable dram on me and asked me to pour it myself because his eyes were troubling him and he didn't like spilling whisky. He has advertised Grant's Standfast in recent years, and everybody told me that the place would be flowing with the stuff. I didn't actually locate the mythical tap bringing the liquor straight from the distillery, but when I poured a tiny tentative tot he was listening, and exhorted me to have a real slug while I was at it.

After ninety years the old man is still shamingly handsome and thinks with all the efficiency of a quartz clock. He lives in a tall house in one of the beautiful Edinburgh squares which are certainly the best town houses anywhere in Britain, and his study gives the impression of having been hollowed out from a cliffside of books and soft old furniture so that no draught has ever been detected in it.

I am not going to try to quote any of his conversation, because the other daunting thing about Mackenzie is his charm, which leaves you in a state of pleasant bemusement in which you can't remember what he actually said, only that it was damned wonderful at the time. And anyway, as I say, he kept encouraging me with the bottle after we got talking about *Walls Have Mouths*.

But for that matter, everybody I know in Edinburgh has worked hard at bemusing Glasgow visitors with liquor, and it has occurred to me that they may all have the idea that Glaswegians do nothing but drink. Or maybe Edinburghers hold that idea as a religious principle, so that they ply Glaswegians with alcohol in order to justify their faith. Edinburghers, when they feel moral, do tut about the nauseating boozing that goes on in Glasgow, and all I can say in rebuttal is that the last time I was in Rose Street, the pavement was so covered with local drunks that I couldn't get room to be sick.

But quite apart from the drink, which is doubtless a show put on for visitors from the West . . . (now that's an interesting possibility. Is it conceivable that Rose Street is simply a front of lath and canvas, pushed into position when a runner comes up from Waverley Station to say that the Glasgow train is in? They could do it easily enough with a few stage-hands and some casters, and the imposing literary figures are no problems either. The ones near the door, which actually speak, are hired actors, wearing false eyebrows and waistcoats with snuff artistically glued down the front; and those at the rear, where the light is dim, are nothing more than pasteboard

The Kenilworth. Rose Street,
Edinb

cutouts, with balloons coming out of their mouths reading, 'I still say the Scottish novel died with George Douglas,' and 'Harewood will never beat back the native philistinism as long as Beaverbrook backs the General Assembly . . .' Many shrewd observers have suspected that Edinburgh Castle itself is a small polythene arrangement which is inflated every morning by a sergeant in the Scots Guards. But no, surely they could never keep a secret that size. Some Edinburgher would blurt it out while he was being injected with booze in Glasgow.) . . . anyway, apart from the drink and the fantasies it provokes, Edinburgh can't possibly be as douce and respectable as it has learned to look.

It's true that Robert Burns lost his head entirely when he went to the Capital, and as a change from bundling in the hay with dairymaids, he wrote in effete English to Mistress Maclehose, the cloth-headed Clarinda of legend. But there's a scrap of conversation somewhere in which the same Rabbie lovingly recalled the Canongate as the place where he bairned two lassies before breakfast. There were wild goings-on, all right. There was Mary Stuart for a start, and if I didn't have an iron will, I would go into the subject of Mary Stuart for the next two hundred pages. Practically everybody else in Scotland has written at least one play about her, and when you think of the Queen of Scots you can see the whole point of Edinburgh. Those old closes, vanishing up or down in flights of stairs into the unseen distance and waiting even now for a Hitchcock team to roll the cameras on them, were built for a city that liked savage dark adventures.

It was only in a city like this that Doctor Jekyll could do his transformation act in fiction, just as Deacon Brodie switched from pillar of society to arch-criminal in real life. The stones are vibrating with old blood that has never cooled.

Deacon Brodie, as all the literate Edinburghers know, was a well-set-up man and a solid citizen who lost too much money at drink and debauchery and became a burglar to keep up his respectable position; a likeable and inoffensive delinquent who was hanged all the same. Most of the best people in Edinburgh died prematurely in the old days.

Mary, Queen of Scots was murdered politically, and I always had a strong prejudice against her because I was brought up a stern Protestant and in addition I became a republican early in life. If there was one thing I couldn't stomach, it was the sentimentalising of forgotten kings and queens, especially Catholics, who were undoubtedly fascist hyenas on the side if not on the front. I would have prescribed long jail sentences for people who wrote plays about Mary and so would every theatre or broadcasting producer in Scotland. Then I found myself reading material on the murder of Henry Darnley, her husband, and I had to fly in the face of principle and take a fancy to the bitch. The truth is that there was no harm in her except that she was a romantic; a fault I have never condemned in *live* young women with nice hair.

Mary lived in Edinburgh in the real, enthusiastic murder age. She was engaged to young Darnley before she ever saw him, and she was daft enough to fall in love with the idea of him before they met. Darnley, the son of a squalid old Polonius of the Scottish aristocracy, had a slim figure and beautiful yellow hair and an emotional age of about seven. He used to hide in his room and drum his heels into the floor when he didn't get what he wanted for breakfast, and if he wasn't a homosexual, he wasn't a kick off it. He arranged the murder of Rizzio, Mary's epicene little personal secretary, out of pique, and later the Earl of Bothwell organised the murder of Darnley to make it even. As a result of all the blood that was being scattered wherever she went, Mary has become spattered with it in people's memories, but that's all a frame-up. The late Brigadier Mahon has done the first unhysterical investigation into the murders and cleared the Queen entirely to my satisfaction.

But what is interesting is that Edinburgh, almost despite itself, has had blood and lust bursting into the open ever since. It is an entirely fitting place to hold an international festival of drama and music.

The Festival is a splendid laugh, not a cynical laugh but hearty. This is the good old Celtic passion for colour and life. It is also a great opportunity for fakes, like me for instance, who can get into the Festival Club and have long loud conversations, based on shorthand notes taken at the Abbotsford in Rose Street, about the fundamentally reactionary philosophy of Fred Shakespeare and the significance of mime in universalising the proletarian drama. When you've had a few, this kind of talk is the berries. You know the man you're talking to is a phoney, and he *knows* you are an illiterate chancer who has never opened a book; but the law of social contract operates, and you both snigger respectfully and feel hellish intellectual.

Deacon Brodie's Tavern,
High street, Edinburgh

The last paragraph merely shows another aspect of the Scottish character. If we enjoy anything too much, we have to deride it in self-defence. In plain terms, the Festival has revived the old blood of Edinburgh, and Scotland. The streets are decorated, and streets *ought* to be decorated. They are filled with strange foreigners, and streets ought to be filled regularly with strange foreigners. The old city feels like a new place, invented overnight for pleasure. You might object that all the plays and concerts and exhibitions in Edinburgh could be discovered individually elsewhere if people were really interested enough; but when the Festival brings them all together, it re-creates a community in which everybody seems to be joining in the same enthusiasm.

The Festival has been running so long that we have all forgotten what a damned dull place Edinburgh could be in September. Suddenly it's a place where you can find Ethel Merman sitting beside you at a table, or Ken Tynan tripping over you as you stoop in the gutter searching for a gold filling. Fervent Scots from other cities have always muttered that Glasgow would be a better place for a festival because there's more culture to the yard in Glasgow all year round than there is in a square mile of Edinburgh. But no other place has that flaming castle and Arthur's Seat and a hilly slope for lovers to lie on, all bang in view of the main street.

The permanent culture of Edinburgh can take some digging, I agree. The second time I ever went to the Festival, some sadist had asked me to look for the Capital's permanent cultural influences, and I went to the Gaiety Theatre in Leith, now gone forever. I can't suggest that it was typical of all of Edinburgh, but it was really something. In Glasgow, you see, a variety hall is expected to go in for a lot of low laughs. In Edinburgh, I discovered that ready tears were called for. In the Leith Gaiety I had one of my cathartic theatrical experiences, which is almost impossible to describe without waving the hands and twisting the features; the features; but I'll try. There was this village green scene, which was definitely the highlight of the show because it had real high-class scenery with a backcloth of the Forth Bridge and cottages on the far side of the river that actually *lit up as night came down*. Where the village green in the foreground came from nobody can tell, since there is no such thing anywhere near that bit of the Firth of Forth, but for God's sake, the theatre means suspension of disbelief, doesn't it? Anyway, there was a lot of jolly village carry-on; no jokes, but a lot of carry-on, which eventually included old Mrs McIvor, tottering up the glen to her wee cottage and lamenting the long absence of her children John and Mary, who had both been away in the Navy for four years without leave. Under Captain Bligh, I suppose.

Finally, the lassie who drove the laundry van offered Mrs McIvor a lift up the glen, which in itself was a high-point of the little drama because it proved that People Are Nice, and the chorus of villagers didn't let anybody forget it. At once, enter John and Mary, merry dance of delight. A rather poignant feature of the drama emerged at this point. John and Mary proposed to spend the night at the village inn, and this was not from mere callousness, but because . . . (here there was a pregnant pause which caught every breath in the stalls) the next day was their dear old mother's birthday, and they were saving themselves up as a surprise.

God help me, you could have heard the audience sighing on the north side of the Firth. I began to feel an alien, because I was sitting in the stalls with Davie Murray, a freelance journalist with very coarse prejudices, who had joined me in the hope of a good belly-laugh, and all round us we could hear the preparatory slurping noises of tear-ducts ready to erupt.

At that very moment, on-stage, the laundry lassie rushed on from the OP side, did a quick take, and then babbled, 'Oh John! Mary!

Princes St. Edinburgh

Er! Your mother! An accident! The van! Up the glen! John! Mary! Accident! Three dots!' (She didn't actually say 'Three dots' out loud. They were part of the business). In a trice, the whole mob had rushed off-stage to view the body, all except for Mary, who was terribly slow off the mark and actually tottered round the stage three times to allow time for a completely new character, the minister, to enter, looking noble and fatherly. Mary, finally cued, made an ineffectual rush to get in among the rubbernecks, but the minister halted her with one outstretched arm and as she stared a choked question into his kindly face, he shook his head sadly and instantly began to shuffle off stage backwards.

The lights came down to a spot, centre, into which Mary hopped, in Wren uniform, and did the whole Eleanora Duse bit for fully thirty seconds, with facial contortions and trembling fingers and everything, and went straight from this warm-up into a good brassy rendering of 'Auld Scots Mither Mine!' Egad, there wasn't a dry eye in the house. Even my own face was streaming, and dreadful

The National Gallery and
the R.S.A., Edinburgh

noises were bursting from me. To cut a long story short, I got thrown out. Politely, but out. It is antisocial to laugh at the sad bits.

This experience does not prove anything in general about Edinburgh. I merely threw it in because I had to get rid of it somehow. It has haunted me long enough. I suppose there must have been some earnest Festival visitors to the Capital that year who would have had more fun down at the Gaiety than they were having with the twelve-tone scale. Every kind of theatre has *something*.

In fact, I bet there are a lot of Festival enthusiasts who would like to see the old Gaiety weepies revived in preference to filthy muck like Shakespeare and those foreign pigs who write about sex and politics and similar garbage. The right-thinking people of Scotland have been massing recently in a crusade to clean the whole thing up, and from their public statements, I imagine the old Gaiety is about their stretch when it comes to genuine human drama.

I use the phrase 'right-thinking people' in a limited sense, by which I mean that that's the phrase they would use themselves. Some funny things have been happening around the Festival recently, and they deserve a good hard look.

Everything at the Festival used to be fine and dandy. Occasionally the ratepayers complained vaguely about the amount of money the whole thing cost, and the Corporation explained that you had to spend a few thousand to attract a million, and the complaints died away for another year. But during 1963, there emerged a more rugged opposition to the idea of unlimited plays and recitals and unrestrained merrymaking.

Just before the Festival that year, I had a glass of wine with Moray McLaren, one of the founder-members of the literary-conversation mob in modern Edinburgh. He had been in hospital recovering from a dose of pneumonia picked up unwittingly in France (serve people right for mixing with those foreigners whose moral turpitude is known to every schoolboy) and he had lain in bed listening for some days to his well-bred Edinburgh neighbours complaining about how much money the Festival lost. Being a cunning man, and determined to take care of his lungs, McLaren smiled his way through all this in silence and prayed for release, but they didn't let him out and he finally had to join in the endless debate.

'The money,' he said, 'is certainly a consideration.' (A nice stylist, McLaren). 'But let us suppose that the Festival made prodigious profits and could be instrumental in *reducing* the city rates.

Insurance
Building:
North Bridge,
Edinburgh

Tenements Partick, Glasgow

You would welcome it then, I presume, and be properly proud of so
businesslike a proceeding.'

Not on your life, they cried aghast. Even if it abolished the rates
altogether, that was no excuse for a lot of jumped-up posers lording
it at symphony concerts and trying to look superior to honest citizens
who were content to watch the telly as their forefathers had done for
centuries.

There's a hard edge there, you see, of the other old Celt, who
knows that God didn't intend other people to have any fun. Especially incomprehensible fun.

Then, at the 1963 Festival, there occurred the great event, or
Happening, that everybody had been waiting for. This took place at
the Drama Conference, a novel entertainment held in the McEwan
Hall, a sonorous circular auditorium forming part of the University.

With my customary unerring instinct, I went to the Conference on
the Day it Didn't Happen. On the platform was a well-mixed collection of theatre folk, occasionally calling one another names, but
usually agreeing rather monotonously about things like the evil of
censorship. The paying customers sat round the hall, the more
extravagant wearing hired earphones through which simultaneous
translations could be heard. It was all very high-minded and well-
intentioned and not much fun, I thought, but live and let live.

On a subsequent day, however, a young American producer,
Kenneth Dewey, livened it up by organising a series of 'Happen-
ings' as a demonstration of instant theatre. These included the
American actress Carroll Baker, in gold tights (gorgeous) clambering
over a row of seats, and a local artists' model, Anna Kesselaar, being
wheeled across the organ gallery, on a trolley, nude. The effect was
surprisingly unsensational, maybe because it happened too quickly.
The people who were really startled were the people who weren't
there at all, and since I wasn't there either, I know how they feel.
If a good-looking lassie is going to appear nude, at least you should
get fair warning so that you can decide to stay away *deliberately*.

Disappointments, however, wear off, and there's always next
year to hope for. But some people weren't content to let disappoint-
ment wear off. When everybody else was wistfully forgetting about
Miss Kesselaar, a prosecution was mounted against her, and she was
summoned to face the charge that she did act in a shameless and
indecent manner, in that she did in full view of those present allow
herself to be wheeled across the organ gallery on a trolley while in a
state of nudity.

At last the staunch regiment of moral Scots had something to go
on; and not only that, Scotland had found a *cause célèbre* as good as
that rotten old Monkey Trial of Darrow's and Jennings'; or the
filthy foreign Dreyfus case. And if you once convict the highbrows of
immorality, you can start from there and sweep out Schoenberg and
Brecht and that shower as well.

A perfectly awful thing happened at the trial, all the same. Anna
was found not guilty. Not only that: the judge, Bailie MacGregor,
opined that a lot of the people who had worked themselves up into a
lather had said things publicly that might have been better left un-
said.

But it wouldn't be fair to suggest that it was Edinburgh that tried
to kill the Festival by nailing Anna Kesselaar. Working behind all the

Castle Wy
Edinb

organised righteousness could be found the subtle hand of a thing called Moral Re-Armament, which you might find just as easily in Duluth, Minnesota, or Frankfurt-am-Main; which proves what I said, that we don't have a monopoly of schizophrenia. In defence of Scotland and its character, I notice that one of the prosecution witnesses in the Kesselaar case, a maiden lady, declared in court that she attended the Drama Conference because she knew the organisers were against censorship, and that this idea 'is contrary to our heritage . . .'

What heritage she meant is obscure, but it couldn't have been the Scottish heritage. We have had plenty of censorship in Scottish history, and religious oppression, and official gags. But the pendulum has always swung against them fast. This is the country where you can't get conformity of thought because half the committee are always walking out and forming a breakaway union, or church, or badminton club. Nobody has ever managed to censor anybody else for very long.

We hear a lot about old John Knox, who has been adopted as patron saint by the anti-fun, pro-censorship lobby recently, and therefore rejected by the pro-fun, anti-censorship lobby. But poor old John wasn't a figure of solid granite. He was just a bloke. It is true that he wanted everybody to conform to his own private vision of the good life, but that vision was highly subversive in its time. He preached his own doctrine of authority because he wanted to throw off the authority of Rome. Knox is not my favourite anarchist, but let us not get him twisted. He was in the front of a movement to throw earthly authority over the wall and deliver spiritual authority into the conscience of every individual man.

Another amiable thing about Knox is that he used his own name and was ready to take the blame for his own convictions. The M R A lads and lasses are curiously coy about coming into the open, and I found this away back in the old days, before they had discovered the anti-Communist crusade; in the old days when they confined themselves to sex with dull fervour, in fact. An old schoolteacher of mine in Glasgow, who had gained the odd impression that I was an eccentric, once organised a meeting at which two other eccentrics and I met three clean-cut morally re-armed young chaps in the Glasgow University Union for a searching of souls to the greater glory of Christ (I *think* it was Christ they were voting for that year). We all had coffee and looked sidewise at one another for a while, and then the First Cheerleader mumbled his way into an exposition of the Four Absolutes, and the greatest of these was purity.

Now it isn't fair to laugh at people whose faith is sincerely held, so we tried not to laugh, until the First Cheerleader got on to the subject of girls, which he was against, we gathered. Deeply conscious of his own impurity, he had devised a cunning penance for himself when the old Adam popped up. Every time he found himself looking at a girl's legs, he turned and walked a hundred paces in the opposite direction.

'What time do you usually get to your classes?' asked McKenzie, one of the eccentrics who was studying medicine and consequently a man without shame or decency. The First Cheerleader looked at us sadly, knowing that we were entrenched in our sin. To be candid, I had a twinge of fear at that moment, in case I might be won over and never more look at girls' legs. What the hell was I going to spend my time looking at? The Second Cheerleader, warmed up to it by this unhealthy excitement, burst in,

'You have to examine your own consciences. When for instance did you last masturbate?'

'You mean in public?' asked Carmichael, who was studying as an engineer, and therefore thought morality was a Dickens novel. The three earnest chaps looked at us, and we looked back at them, all demonstrating the Fourth Absolute, which was Absolute Hate, I think. At the time, none of us eccentrics smoked or drank, which in our opinion made us fairly high-class moral citizens, but we walked halfway home staring at girls' legs like billy-o. It was marvellous. None of this is very relevant to anything, so to return to the Edinburgh Festival, there was an MRA conference a few days before Christmas, 1963, at which a resolution was passed calling for Festivals free of filth, poetry of pornography, and drama free of dirt. 'The Conference', it added, 'rejects the McCarthyite mentality of those who would debase our festivals, theatres, broadcasting channels and weekly newspapers.' I appreciated the word McCarthyite, since Mr McCarthy, the honest soul, is best remembered for his Communistic opposition to censorship.

The best filth I ever had in Edinburgh was when I wallowed into the documents in the case that has been described as Scotland's greatest criminal cause, and which really ought to be censored retrospectively because it could easily lead to necrophilia if allowed to lie naked (naked!) on library shelves. It is the story of Burke and Hare.

At the Grassmarket
Edinburgh

There's no doubt that the best way to put a town on the map is to produce a body, and if you have to make sure, get a whole heap of the things. William Burke and William Hare, in their own time, were merely small tradesman trying to get ahead. The fame which they brought to Edinburgh is only a by-product they never intended, and if they had, they would have asked for royalties.

Burke and Hare are remembered inaccurately as the body-snatchers. But in truth, neither of them ever belonged to the respectable trade of body-snatching, which had been practised in the Edinburgh district (and elsewhere, of course) long before their rollicking time. The reason why Edinburgh has to take all the smears for this industry is simply that Scotland's capital city was a notable pioneer in the science of medicine, which required bits of human corpse for serious study as soon as it emerged from the magic-pass,

NORTH GRAY'S CLOSE

A closemouth gossip
on The Royal Mile, Edinburgh

boiled-toads'-eye stage. As early as 1505, Edinburgh granted a char-
ter to the Incorporation of Surgeons and Barbers, requiring every
entrant to study the anatomy of the human body, and for this pur-
pose the Incorporation was given an allowance of one corpse per
year; that of a condemned criminal after he had been thoroughly
hanged.

Inevitably, there wasn't enough body to go round, and the ration
was increased in 1694 to include various categories of unwanted
departed.

But anatomical study had caught on, and everybody was clamour-
ing for cadavers, and by the beginning of the eighteenth century,
Edinburgh's graveyards were beginning to look like small quiet zoos,
with iron cages built over the lairs to discourage the new industry of
resurrectionism. Conscientious students stole freshly-buried corpses
as a matter of honour. Later, private enterprise crept in, and skilled
specialists worked full-time at exhuming specimens to sell to the
anatomical classrooms. There was even a long-distance commerce in
the commodity. Bodies were exported from London to satisfy Edinburgh's incessant demand. Even today, I may say, Scotland is badly
off for dissectable corpses because few Scots are prepared to be cut
up even after death.

You might say that it was the natural law of supply and demand
that created Burke and Hare. Neither partner was an Edinburgher,
by the way. Like my own forebears, they were born in Ireland and
came to Scotland as the land of promise. Their story is quite modern,
by historical standards. Both were born in the 1790's, and their formal career didn't start until 1827.

Burke was a reasonable-enough little man to look at, nimble and
well-co-ordinated, and a good natural dancer. Hare was a pretty
repulsive character on the outside, but his brutish exterior concealed
an ordinary, unpretentious monster.

A chain of casual incidents provided the means of the business
the two men later founded. Hare, when he came to Scotland, worked
on the Union Canal (nothing of any size in Scotland would ever have
been built without the labour of low-class Irish exiles), and while
working as a labourer, he met a man called Logue, who kept a tramps'
lodging-house in Tanner's Close, in Edinburgh. Logue had a
woman, Margaret Laird. Hare became a lodger in the house, and was
thrown out after fighting with Logue, but Logue himself died in
1826.

Laird, the bereaved doxy, took one of the young lodgers as an interim mate, but Hare returned and established himself as the new master, happily settled with a woman of his own and a profitable establishment. It was a fairly desperate establishment, with eight beds, The lodgers paid 3d a night for a share of a bed. Very soon, they included William Burke and the life-partner he had acquired, Helen McDougal. The relationship was casual enough, since Burke had a wife and children back in Ireland and McDougal had two husbands still living. But it lasted, bolstered by a common passion for booze and business.

Late in 1827, an old man died in the lodging house, owing Hare £4 in rent, and the landlord thought he might be able to sell the corpse to recover the debt. He confided in his lodger Burke, and the two together prised open the coffin, filled it with rubbish, and hid the body. That night they visited the rooms of the celebrated Doctor Robert Knox and after some shilly-shallying, revealed that they had a specimen for sale. A bargain was struck, the body was delivered, and the lads were paid £7 10s.

Visions of wealth swam before them. Edinburgh was seething with feeble people who could easily be converted into saleable stuff, and Burke and Hare started to comb the streets for likely subjects. But their real wealth was ready to hand. They had a lodging-house. One of the other lodgers fell ill of a fever, and while he was too weak to protest, the boys held a pillow over his face till he died.

Another lodger went through the same routine on contracting jaundice. After this, the partnership developed a technique for attracting fresh business. An old beggar woman was decoyed to Tanner's Close for a drink. She drank herself blind and stayed the night, and in the morning, when they were sober enough to manage it, Hare pressed his hand over her nose and mouth while Burke lay across her body to keep her calm. They packed the body in a tea-chest and delivered it to a porter, sent by Dr Knox, at the back of the Castle.

The fresh corpses fetched £10, and Burke and Hare became regular suppliers. It isn't possible to give a precise count of the victims, because the company didn't keep books, but there were certainly at least sixteen. This was not body-snatching or resurrectionism. The specimens from Tanner's Close were freshly killed on the premises.

Some of the ventures were unusually gruesome, even in this con-

Stephen Cargill, a painter

text. In April of 1828, Burke was drinking in Swanston's in the Canongate when two teenage girls came in. They were Mary Paterson and Janet Brown, and both were prostitutes, but Mary Paterson was particularly noticeable as a raving beauty. Burke saw at once that she would make a beautiful corpse. He bought the lassies several drinks and invited them back 'to his lodgings', and all three went to the house of Burke's brother, Constantine, a more or less honest scavenger. Mary Paterson was soon dead drunk, but Janet kept her wits.

Suddenly Burke's floozie, Helen McDougal, burst in on them and accused Janet of trying to seduce her husband, and after a noisy exchange, Janet left the house. She returned later for her friend, and found Hare, who told her that Mary had gone out with Burke and would soon be back. Mary in fact was lying dead under a sheet on the bed while they spoke. Hare, with his usual reckless charm, offered her more drink, but she left, without being smothered, and stayed alive.

The arrival of Mary's corpse on Knox's dissecting table caused a small sensation, because several of the anatomy students had known her by sight, and the pupils crowded round to admire the splendid proportions of the body. Several of them sketched it, and others wanted to know how this glorious young woman had died. Burke said she had died of drink, and nobody was prepared to question this.

Another harrowing case was that of an old Irishwoman, searching for relatives in Edinburgh, and escorting her grandson of twelve, a boy who had been dumb from birth. Burke promised to find the missing relatives, took her to Tanner's Close, and in the back room, he and Hare prepared her for delivery. Next morning the quartette discussed what they might do with the little boy, and thought of taking him out and losing him. But since this might have caused inquiries, Burke bowed to necessity, took the child into the back room where the dead grandmother lay, and laying the victim across his knee, he broke his back.

Burke said later that the piteous expression of the wistful eyes of this boy haunted him; which seems reasonable enough.

The business was going so smoothly now that the partners grew reckless. One of their later subjects was Daft Jamie, a harmless idiot who was familiar to everybody in Edinburgh. Jamie was lured in the routine way to the lodging-house, but failed to get helpless drunk, and fought savagely to defend himself before Burke and Hare managed to finish their business. He was instantly recognised by students when he arrived on the table, and one of the points raised against Dr Knox later was that the surgeon, who usually took bodies in the order of their arrival, ordered this one to be dissected at once. The obvious distinguishing marks were thus destroyed.

The enterprise finally fell to pieces on a Hallowe'en night when

Burke met a garrulous little Irishwoman, Mrs Docherty, in search of her relatives like so many other transients in Edinburgh at the time. Burke exclaimed in delight that his own mother's name was Docherty and that they must be related, and took her to his own house for the night. He had a couple of lodgers at the time, James Gray and his wife, and since Burke's room was too small for a big party, the Grays agreed to lodge with Mrs Hare for the night and leave space.

Next morning, the Grays came back to Burke's room for breakfast, and found the little Irishwoman gone. Burke explained that the visitor had become a nuisance and had been kicked out, but when Mrs Gray started looking round the room for her child's stockings, Burke brusquely ordered her away from a heap of straw near the bed. Burke behaved very oddly as the day went on, and in the late afternoon, while he was out, Mrs Gray decided to investigate the room. Under the straw she discovered the corpse of Mrs Docherty.

Fleeing from the murder house, the Grays met Helen McDougal and told her about the body. McDougal begged them to keep quiet about it, and promised that their silence would be worth £10 a week to them, but the Grays, who were certainly in need of money, turned her down and went to the police.

The trial of Burke and Hare was widely held to be a disastrous miscarriage of justice at the time. Nobody had any doubt about the volume of their guilt, but the prosecution found that their case was dismally weak for lack of evidence, and Hare was offered immunity for turning King's Evidence. This also let his woman off. To make sure of a verdict, the prosecution confined the indictment to three murders – Jamie, Mary Paterson and Mrs Docherty. But in a complex business of legalistic ping-pong, a verdict was brought in only on the Docherty case. Burke was found guilty and the charge against McDougal was Not Proven.

Doctor Knox was ruined. The three lucky partners tried to vanish from public savagery, and finally did. William Burke was sentenced to death, and the Lord Justice Clerk ordered that he be hanged on January 28, 1829, and that his body be 'publicly dissected and anatomised.'

'And I trust,' the judge added, 'that if it is ever customary to preserve skeletons, yours will be preserved, in order that posterity may keep in remembrance your atrocious crimes.'

The body is in a showcase in the Anatomical Museum of Edinburgh University.

THE FIRST
SHAMBLING FOOT

Life in old Caledonia is getting all smoothed over with supermarkets and television and Daylight Saving, but in spite of all this, we are still all rugged and anthropological underneath. We have adopted the English Christmas which was invented by a German prince, but it's still a pale imitation thing compared with our own old pagan rite of Hogmanay. My splendid American dictionary says that Hogmanay is the Scottish New Year's Eve, when children go about singing and soliciting gifts. But they don't, not where I come from. The best thing about Hogmanay is that it's one festival from which we have managed to exclude brats entirely. It is strictly an adult squalor.

Earlier in this century, that dictionary description was probably true enough. Before the Christmas business managed to infiltrate Scottish folklore, kids got their presents at New Year, when there was anything going. But since they have manufactured the big Christmas gouge, we have cut them out of Hogmanay altogether.

This assertion of the rights of adults, in defiance of the mainstream of history, is the envy and the admiration of the world, and it's not surprising that it has been frenziedly copied by other nations, to the extent where Anglo-Saxons jump into fountains in London as midnight strikes. And it's one of the traditions of which we can rightly be proud. If children are allowed into everything, they have no incentive for growing up.

There was no mawkish concession to child-worship in my ancestral home. Hogmanay was a totally forbidden delight, and the tiny tots were clamped down in their little beds good and early to dream of the delicious orgies that were not for them. My early recollection of New Year's Eve is of nights spent in dark uneasy sleep, unnerved by the total silence from downstairs and interrupted at some nameless hour by the discovery that I would die if I didn't get up and go to the lavatory. It was only on Hogmanay that this desperate need wakened me in the night, and the sharp painful urgency is what childhood Hogmanays mean to me.

The total silence from downstairs may seem curious, but that's the way it happened in my home, and in most others, until the very stroke of midnight. We've gone a bit decadent nowadays, and craven Scots will yield to the torment of flesh and start having a sneaky nip at nine o'clock in the evening; but when I was finally old enough to be allowed to stay up for the bells, there was no self-indulgence of that kind. The bottle and the shortbread and the black bun were on the sideboard, but they were next year's delights, and we had to go clean and sober over the threshold of the year.

Clean, sober and without sin or obligation. The evening of Hogmanay is spent in merciless house-cleaning so that no speck of dirt will be carried into another era. A genuine Scot will not even allow a small bill to go unpaid from one year into another. There is still a mad scramble at official counters to settle rent and rates and fuel bills before the bell tolls, and at the last possible moment of the old year, the fire is carefully raked and the ashes are taken out to the dustbin to make quite sure.

Latterly, with all the mob of brothers and sisters scattered to their own homes, and the old man three thousand miles away for the tenth or eleventh year, the vigil would be kept by my mother and the remaining infants, myself and one or two brothers at the tail-end of the tribe. It was a situation tailor-made for melancholy, but in any family, there will always be a tinge of melancholy. The eruption of sadness was sternly suppressed in a frenzy of cleaning and polishing, and held back through the last tingling minutes until a window was raised to let in the sound of the church bells. Then one of us would pour the port – the old lady had a phase when nothing but Graham's three-star would suit the occasion – and before we drank we would accept her kisses, already verging on damp fervour, and shake hands and toast a Guid New Year. Then she would stand a heave a long sigh and impatiently dash away the flooding tears. We wanted to be impatient of the tears too, because Hogmanay was supposed to be dandy fun and the time for looking forward to new excitements; but we accepted the tears as proper and legitimate and felt them coming

too. She would have a wee quiet drink to her only brother Jimmy,
gone to Canada when she was still only a girl, the protector of her
orphan childhood whom she was sure she would never see again, and
we would feel the terrible sadness of the years that take everything
away. And we would drink to the old man, who had gone to America
in '28 to prepare a new life for us all. He had done it, too, but somehow my mother's nerve failed when it came to pulling up her roots,
and the years slipped away and we never went, and he never came
back, and now we never would, and he never would. My God, Hogmanay was a lacerating experience, for all the joy and the booze. Then
we would have a few more from the bottle of three-star and the old
years would be washed away and we could believe that 1938 or 1939
would be the best year that ever happened.

By the time the new year was an hour old, the old lady would be

Near Beauly

in love with everybody, calling people toads in a tone of indulgent menace, and slapping you on the back without warning so that your spine rattled. The first-foot would have arrived and the night would be swinging.

The first-foot is the bringer of fortune, the blessing on the house, the emissary of the fates and the test of hospitality and friendship. He must be a man, never a woman, and he should be dark, never blond or red-haired. He must bear the gifts of good cheer and receive them. A lump of coal has become *de rigeur* among some first-footers as the symbol of good luck, but this is a pretty poor token on its own if he doesn't bring good Scotch whisky as well, to give drink and receive it. An old Irishwoman once told me that in her village, the head of the house welcomed the New Year by flinging a loaf of bread at the door, but I would never try that because you never know who might get it in the kisser, and not many people have the stability to survive such a surprise on New Year's morning.

For years my oldest brother Harry would first-foot us because he had all the qualifications. One year, when he was a few minutes late, we had a red-haired man held at bay on the doorstep freezing to death and trying to convince us that the black-haired legend was a load of old boots, because he was frantic to get in beside the fire and start the booze-up. But we weren't standing for any confidence-tricks of that kind. He damn well froze until the ceremony had been performed by a proper blackhead.

The festering ambition of the growing child was of course to assume full manhood and be a first-foot, instead of sitting there waiting for one. One of the reasons why New Year celebrations become endless and chaotic is that you're liable to be out combing the streets trying to first-foot people who are out combing the streets first-footing other people. The Scots have always been early bedders and none of your night-club nonsense, and this has always been the one night of all when the nation has a licence to be up turning night into day, so it can be pure hell. The first-foot you expected has met other first-footers and exchanged greetings and swigs from the bottle and quite possible been seduced into swelling somebody else's raiding party, and you have gone to bed in disgust at 4 a.m. to be wakened by loathsome drunken friends kicking the door at seven in the morning and yelling resentfully up at your windows. If they take the spirit of New Year seriously, they will not have confined themselves to visiting people they know. Any house with lights showing is liable to bring out the tearful, brithers-be-for-a'-that fervour of their besotted Scotch natures, and they may have spent half the night speechless drunk under a stranger's table.

In theory, this is the time when every Scotsman re-discovers his love for the whole of humanity, and the theory works well enough. What often makes Hogmanay memorable is the way our frail natures break down. One New Year, in the wild madness of youth, I was doing the rounds with a girl I very much fancied in defiance of her old man's hostility – not every girl's parents loved me as I deserved, and in that sense I had a normal, invigorating adolescence – when a dim figure appeared passing a nearby lamp-post. The girl, her caution obliterated by two dry sherries, shouted 'Dad!' in maudlin affection, and in a few seconds the Dad was breathing Black Label round us and swimming up through his Ne'erday good-humour to

The Citizens Theatre, Glasgow

recognise the black-hearted villain who was trying to get his innocent daughter drunk. This accusation left me speechless because it was true, so I reached in my pocket to offer him a cigarette, because that's how people always smoothed things down in the movies.

'Draw a gun on me, will you!' he babbled, and swung a neat left hook that missed me by less than a foot. The last I saw of my New Year plans was the old boy being hustled for home by a convenient son, with his beautiful daughter trying to shush his curses, and me standing there with nearly a full bottle of sherry and nobody to ply with it. However, a man with one leg – honestly – appeared out of the darkness and dragged me off to a house with friendly, likkered-up parents and four daughters and about thirty other people, and I was able to spend the rest of the night looking tragic and interesting and being kissed by middle-aged aunties – the daughters were all booked, it goes without saying.

A permanent crisis of the Hogmanay orgy was the presence in the world of the Joiners. No matter how carefully and how long you planned in advance to set up a small, amiable sortie of first-footers, balanced as to temperament and to sex, some excessive clinger would try to join on and ruin the night by laughing at the wrong jokes and being sick on you or holding you by the jacket and talking about politics while you and a girl were trying to hide in the lobby and drink out of the neck of the same bottle as a love-token. The economic law of the Additional Man is not exclusively Scots, I suppose, but it happened so often here that we thought we had invented it. If you decide to hold a party in a telephone box, to guarantee its exclusiveness, one of the people in the box will turn out to be Additional.

One year out in Shettleston at the East End of Glasgow, which was a splendid place for first-footing because everybody knew everybody by sight at least and there could never be a shortage of houses to knock at, we had a tidy foursome organised when an Additional Man pleaded to be allowed to join us out of his unpopulated darkness. We promised to take him to the first house on the list and he agreed to abandon us there, but five drinks and three houses later he was still there, everywhere. He was the kind of masculine big bloke who gets maudlin instantly and spills things, and it took over an hour of muttered conversations and a lung-searing chase through the closes and back courts of Parkhead before we shook him off. We were perfectly callous about it because by nature he would assuredly find another innocent little group and limpet on to it.

In glorious freedom, all exchanging kisses and handshakes impartially, we ducked into the nearest house on the list, where terrible things happened and were clearly a judgment on us. It was the grim time of the dread whisky shortage, and we were punished not by the home-made wine we were offered (it looked like milky tea and tasted of prunes) but by the fact that it had been spiked with genuine illicit alcohol. Our host had an acquaintance who, I solemnly swear, had built and operated an illicit still in a ground-floor room-and-kitchen in a four-storey tenement at Parkhead. Reckless with triumph, I knocked off a tumblerful of this beige fortified plonk, and at once passed into Cheyne-Stokes breathing and lurched into a corner to die.

A curious Hogmanay tradition is the custom of being married on New Year's Eve. This is not a question of being wed accidentally while sloshed, but deliberate pre-planning, and it dates from the time when working people had few holidays and could use the time off at New Year for a honeymoon, if they were able to remember it later. It isn't any sillier than most marriage customs. In living memory, marriages in rural Aberdeenshire have been signalised by barbaric Nordic drinking fests and communal defloration – I use the

Latin expression to avoid unhealthy stimulation of any foreign reader.

Later, when I was married, we celebrated Hogmanay like decent housebound folk, and none of your adolescent nonsense here, holding hands is the absolute limit. Hogmanay continued to be gloriously unpredictable, nevertheless. We lived in a vast old ground-floor flat in Hillhead with a big basement, and practically anybody, native or imported, might fall through the front door. There was one pregnant moment when we were holding a quiet, intellectual New Year gathering in the big room upstairs, and I excused myself for a moment to refill a water-jug, or something. As I crossed the hall, I saw what was obviously the tail-end of a great crocodile of total strangers stumbling downstairs to the basement.

'Er, uhuh, eh?' I said, always the gentleman, and the tail-end Charlie turned round with an oafish smile and said, 'It's all right, we know the people that live here.'

Long after we had dismissed the last guest that night, by oxtering him to the front door and pushing him in the small of the back, we heard a taxi stopping outside the house, and as we lay there in the dark with a tender babe asleep beside us, we knew without question that the mumbling reveller who fell out of the taxi was heading in our direction. I sailed out of bed in one desperate movement to get the great front door opened and fend him off before he could waken the child, but I was still fumbling with the bolt when he started hammering from outside and the wean started yelling.

'Hullo!' he said, dead narked. 'Ziss a place wherezzz a party? Hey? Come oan, let me in. Ziss McClure's hoose, eh? innit?'

'Sssh!' I shouted at him, at his disgusting beery face and his unknown figure and his revolting personality, a man who drank alcohol and molested innocent, good-living citizens.

'Hey, a good New Year, err, Mac!' he shouted. 'Come on, lemme in, I know r's a party, come on, this is McClure's, innit?'

'Sssh!' I screamed. 'You've got the wrang hoose, McClure's is on the other side.'

'Aw, don't come it! Ah know the number a' right, you canny kid me, come on, let us in, Mac, they know me a'right.'

'It's across the street,' I said. 'That green door.'

He swayed on the top step and peered across the street.

'Helluva funny, that. Helluva funny.' And he meant that I was helluva funny, and not to be trusted, with my trick of moving houses

Gorbals Cross, Glasgow

to the wrong side of the street. But he had already staggered three steps downwards as he turned, and I put my shoulder against the door and got the bolt home.

I would have been better to take him in. Things were really humming at the McClures, and they lived one storey up, and there wasn't a hope of anybody hearing a doorbell. The mysterious stranger started by ringing their bell, and we lay in bed and listened to this. Then we lay in bed and listened to him thinking, in a slow and disconnected manner, and then we lay and listened to him kicking the downstairs door.

The tender babe, having realised that the noise was merely an ordinary drunk man, went happily back to sleep, and we spent a pleasant forty minutes anticipating every move of the rejected wanderer.

'He'll look for stones to chuck at the window,' Anna told me. There was the ring of pebbles on glass.

'He'll look for a half-brick next,' I whispered. There was the long silence of a man looking for a half-brick and not finding one.

'He'll start kicking.' He started kicking.

'He'll scream.'

He screamed.

'Hey, Jackie! Jackie Green!' It was a pitiful wail, the cry of a waif who has lost his nannie.

'Let me in, Jackie! Jackie Green. Aw, *Jackie*!'

Pitiful. The intrusion of the name of Jackie Green was puzzling until we surmised that the night visitor didn't actually know the McClures, but had been invited by one of their guests. That's how parties grow.

'Hey, Jackie!' This time the pitiful note had been abandoned, and he was hectoring, sergeant-major style. 'Green! Open this door! . . . Aw, come on, Jackie! I know you're there.'

He was still sobbing and kicking as we fell into a dreamless sleep.

National customs have become so diluted, so widely imitated, corrupted and borrowed back by the original owners, that I had begun to think in recent years that the old magic of Hogmanay was illusory, and that there was nothing particularly Scotch left in it. I was wrong, but it was fun finding out. We did this in the deep Highlands at Aviemore.

'New Year's a dead loss,' Anna said to me cunningly one October. 'We should go away for a holiday and abandon it.'

On holiday, away from home and loved ones at Hogmanay? My mother would have classed such a move as a sacrilege, and the idea was so blasphemous that my heart leapt at the sound of it. We began to tell each other how rational it was, to disappear and be no longer the prey of any drunk passerby (we hadn't had a drunk passerby for years since we moved to a respectable district). We spoke of the joy of having no glasses broken, no louts vomiting on the carpet (a phenomenon we barely remembered) and no cleaning-up to do on New Year's Day.

Down with the corruption of drink and wassail, we decided. We would go for a healthy, rigorous ski-ing holiday and enjoy the clear-eyed frugal healthy life. So we packed the brats and some thick underwear and headed North, and the kids betrayed themselves as puerile non-traditionalists. They were delirious.

Quite apart from traditions and New Year, ski-ing is a great game in Scotland now. It goes with such a bang that people have wondered why it never happened before, and why everybody had to go to Switzerland or Norway for the slalom nonsense. The reason is that nobody in Scotland ever had any money. I mean, most people never had any money. The curse of Scotland has always been quite simply poverty for too many people, and the other thing that is bred by generations of poverty – a refusal to enjoy anything that looks uppish, even if it isn't actually expensive. If there is a deficiency in the Scottish character (and by God, there is) it's the turnip-faced conviction that some pleasures are legitimate because they've always been there, but others are affected and obnoxious because they are used exclusively by foreigners and pansified toffs to show off.

This isn't class-consciousness in the English sense, though it may be a similar thing in reverse. The English idea of class has never really got off the ground in Scotland, the system whereby an accent and a school fixes a man for all time in one narrow layer of humanity arranged by God. In general, Scotsmen take it for granted that any slum brat can and will end up as the boss of ICI or, if he hasn't the smeddum for that, as Prime Minister. If he does, the lumpen Scot will applaud him, and only the narks who are found in all races will say, as somebody said of George Blake 'Famous? Him? Away you go, I kent his faither.'

And if the slummie who has got to the top cares to go in for ocean yacht races or scooshing down the Cresta Run, his old neighbours will feel a complacent pride in him.

But it's different for the other slummie down the street, who has *not* become the boss of I C I, and is still there to be seen in the flesh. He's in danger of being regarded as cheeky if he goes ski-ing or sailing, or becomes a champion fencer.

Swimming is all right. Running the Marathon is all right. For some odd reason, Judo is all right. These are comprehensible healthy pursuits for ordinary buddies. Golf and tennis are still a bit on the cheeky side, badminton is definitely putting it on. Getting boozed was good enough for the old man, it should be good enough for you. That is how Scottish chauvinism has worked, narrowing life down to a sullen insistence on simple joys and lasting tedium. It has taken a few stubborn pioneers and the postwar generation of arrogant youth, greedy for experience, to sweep it away.

While I'm writing this, it occurs to me that mountain-climbing is a surprising exception, and the reason is that it developed from the old Socialist enthusiasm for rambling and cycling and the cheap open air. Climbing in Scotland was always an extremely high-class pastime until a crowd of unemployed shipyard workers in Clydebank formed the Creagh Dhu club during the depression of the thirties. Climbing got them because all the equipment they needed was a sandwich and a pair of sand-shoes. The hard-muscled toughs of the Creagh Dhu were not the only good climbers in Scotland, but they helped to open up a lot of the great climbs, and they and the University climbers quickly overturned the precious classifications of some of the classic climbs. Ascents that had been marked Very Severe in the guide-books were down-graded to Easy Strolls for Ladies by these boys.

Some of them once roped me and led me up the Chimney on the Cobbler, which used to be regarded as pretty big stuff, and if they could make me do it first time, they could do anything.

I started this off by girning at the Scottish passion for never doing anything different, but there is a nonsensical Scottish climbing tale that makes me look a fool, and I must put it down in case I forget it later.

During the period when Sir John Hunt was getting ready to make the conquest of Everest, two unknown Scottish toughs, John Cunningham and Hamish MacInnes, decided that they would have a go at the thing themselves. Hunt, very wisely and efficiently, organised his go on the conventional lines of a well-equipped military operation, with food and clothes scientifically tested and oxygen and Sherpas and everything else available. He made it, and jolly good luck to him.

Cunningham was a member of Creagh Dhu. MacInnes, whom I never met, was known as a lone wolf, who sometimes climbed with the club but never joined anything. According to Cunningham, from whom I got the story, MacInnes was a lout of great and irresistible charm, who on any expedition always ended up in the best sleeping-bag and with most grub, and nobody ever knew how he had swung it on them yet again.

The two of them with their insolent notion of beating the Himalayas, started off on the realistic basis of being broke. They didn't even have their fares to India, so they signed on for assisted emigrant passages to New Zealand for the first step, intending to work hard enough there to work off their debt to the Government and then plan the next step. Eventually they were able to leave New Zealand on a cheap boat for India with about thirty pounds to finance their idiotic adventure.

Once in India, they bummed and hitch-hiked their way to Nepal, had the usual trouble about getting in and flannelled their way through. They had written begging letters to all sorts of suppliers of equipment, offering a magnificent endorsement in return when they came home victorious, and as far as I recollect, the only people who answered them were a chocolate company and a film manufacturer, so that they were confident of being able to take plenty of pictures of each other eating chocolate. In fact, when they got into the foothills of the Himalayas, they found a peasantry so poor that nobody would even sell them food, and they lived for some days on turnips stolen from fields. In this condition, and without oxygen or bearers or any encouragement, they decided to leave Everest to the big battalions, but they got to the top of Pingaro, the Finger, which is well over twenty-thousand feet. And they came back to tell the tale, but not many people have heard it, and there were no knighthoods attached to it either.

This does not alter the fact that the simple Scot, until recent years, regarded ski-ing as a photogenic idiocy, confined to the movies and nobs, and a Glasgow prole in the thirties who proposed to spend Hogmanay sliding down mountains on two planks would have excited pity and derision, if not actually a clout on the chops. We have therefore progressed far into modern times when the idea provokes nothing but envy and congratulations.

It isn't quite as tidy, this Scottish ski-ing, as people imagine Switzerland to be. The ski-lifts are sprouting, but they hadn't started working when we were there a couple of years ago, and you sometimes have to travel some miles to find a bit of snow if you go as early as December. But on the day we arrived at Aviemore, teeming rain was reported from the Swiss Alps, and two days later we had a twelve-inch fall of snow in the village of Aviemore itself. Within another two days, the temperature in the district was minus sixteen Fahrenheit, or minus twenty-seven Centigrade; a shade colder than Moscow at the same time.

Ski-ing is very nearly the best thing that has happened to the ordinary Scotsman. It invogorates the body and liberates the spirit, and I found that even as I fell on to the battered right hip for the twentieth time, I could convince myself that I was living like a god. After the snow fell on the village, of course, my little tribal group gave up travelling miles in a bus, and worked on the terraced lawn beside the hotel. In no time my son, an arrogant teenager if you ever

By the River Ness:
    Alistair McDonald and his bike

saw one, had taught himself to do little jumps without ski-sticks, and
was exhorting me to do them too, by sneering at my grey hairs.

Oh, the healthy frugal open-air life was the joy all right. We
could spend a whole morning with ice forming on our eyebrows and
then ski right down to the front of the hotel and fall through the bar
entrance in one gliding movement.

The traditional Hogmanay outbreak was going to be no problem
either. A hotel is full of bedrooms and lounges and central heating,
and you can first-foot till the dawn without ever getting your nose
cold. It was noticeable that the genuine old ascetic tradition of keeping the bottle corked till midnight had vanished, but it is vanishing
everywhere. An atmosphere of painful excitement burgeoned as the
hours ticked away, because the guests included a great mob of bright,
healthy young schoolteachers from the North of England, spending
their very first Hogmanay in the land that invented it. Great goings-
on were to be expected all round.

There were great goings-on, all right. A small huddled knot of
Scots, swollen by one rather desperate Corsican, sneaked off to an
empty lounge as the magic hour approached, and we brought in the
New Year very much as I had once brought it in with my mother

and my brothers, except that two of our under-age children had fought their way into the celebration, and I was the one who paused to feel sad about the passing of time.

We produced our bottles and ceremonially exchanged drinks, hailing Cesar the Corsican as a Scotsman and being accepted in return as bandits. Everything started on this quiet, reverential note, which is correct. As each member present insisted on a round from his bottle, the little group grew noisier and more creative. Athletic people, carried away with bonhomie, stood on their hands. Non-pianists tried a tune on the baby grand. Ancient tunes were dredged up from the collective unconscious. We certainly sang,

> Three craws
> Sat upon a wa'
> Sat upon a wa'
> Sat upon a wa'
> Three craws
> Sat upon a wa'
> On a cold and frosty morning.
>
> First wee craw
> couldny flee at a'
> On a cold and frosty morning
>
> Next wee craw
> Fell and broke his jaw
> On a cold and frosty morning.
>
> Third wee craw
> Went to teel his maw
> On a cold and frosty morning.
>
> Fourth wee craw
> Wisnae there at a'
> On a cold and frosty morning.

And so, with many a song and frivolity, we were set to wheel the night away, when some of the keen young English teachers – all in their early twenties – came timidly through the door, and were welcomed in the true Hogmanay spirit by being offered a drink. Some of them didn't take it, and a human being is entitled not to drink. But steeped in tradition as we were, we all noticed simultaneously that whether they drank or not, none of them had caught on to the infrangible rule that *you bring a drink with you.*

In twos and threes they crowded in, and a most hideous thing happened. They sat down on the floor, in rows, like pupils or paying customers, and waited for the entertainment to proceed. They must have heard that Scotsmen are a load of fun on Hogmanay, and they had booked their seats to observe it. When I left the room to deliver a noggin to some absent friend, I came back to find the door jammed shut by a press of sitting bodies, and a group of earnest Sassenachs barring it to me because, they said, the place was too crowded for anybody else to get in.

A place too crowded, on Hogmanay ?

'Aroint the lot of youse, you po-faced loons, and a murrain on your pallid sweetbreads,' I snarled at them, and scrunched across their outstretched fingers to rejoin the beleaguered garrison, and we stared at each other, two communities utterly alienated, till they found it was their bedtime and went by-byes.

Then we passed a bottle round again, and felt a quiet, sniggering satisfaction creeping through us. We were the guardians of a tradition, and we were damn well going to guard it against all comers. All comers, that is, who were too barbarous to know what was expected of them.

BOATS

It must be a strange and terrible thing to live on a Russian steppe or a Kansas prairie, and never hear the sound of the sea. A Canadian I know who was brought up in Saskatoon recalls that he used to get into his car every weekend and drive two hundred miles through the dust to look at a puddle, and then drive back home refreshed. In Scotland, if you shut your eyes and take a running jump, you'll end up in deep water, and that's the way it ought to be.

It isn't only that all life came originally from the sea. Man himself was probably an amphibian quite recently in evolutionary time. That's why we have no fur. When we said goodbye to the trees and took to the water, the only place we needed hair was on top, to keep the sun off and fool the pterodactyls into thinking that we were clumps of weed or floating coconuts.

We are therefore creatures who need an occasional sight of the sea in order to feel reassured that we haven't got completely lost. Even far inland in Glasgow, the oceans of the world reach up along the River Clyde to comfort us. The great shipbuilding cranes on the riverbanks, visible for miles, keep us in touch with our unconscious past. The Scots, it goes without saying, invented the principle of seaside holidays. The Clyde Coast was the first People's Playground because it was *there*.

The river opens out into a salt-water Firth sprinkled with islands and sheltered by hills, and busy with boats since long before Henry Bell's *Comet* chugged downriver as the first commercial power vessel in the world. Clyde connoisseurs used to show their skill by recognising every one of the fleet of pleasure steamers at a glance from

Largs

" Clyde - built "

three miles. Non-connoisseurs were content to feel themselves aboard a boat. Trains are fine in their way, but the second you step on a steamer your holiday has really begun. The father of the family would stand on deck as the boat slid down the river and classify every half-built hull on the shipyard stocks for the education of his children, and he would do this whether he knew anything about them or not, because no Scottish father will confess ignorance on any point relating to boats or ships. Then, as the river broadened and the salt sharpened the air, he would breathe deeply and say he was going down to have a look at the engines. I used to think people *were* going to look at the engines. I hadn't realised that this was yet another Scottish code-phrase for ducking into the bar.

It seemed logical to look at the engines literally. A paddle-steamer's engines are titanic machines, with hundredweights of cam and great cranks as thick as a man, shining silver and smelling of sweet hot oil. But drinking on a steamer is also dangerously alluring, heave-ho me hearties and yo ho ho and a bottle of rum. There was one steamer with a little bar buried so deep in its hull that you could look through the plate-glass ports and see green water; and a sight like that can give a man a terrible urgent thirst.

At the end of this, there are still more boats. The basic Scottish boat is the clinker pulling dinghy – I throw this description in with a simper, and take my place with every Scotsman who has to plaster his talk with technical nonsense. I never called it anything but a boat. No man is a man, and no boy is a man, who hasn't hired a boat and rowed it round and round Rothesay Bay, or up and down the Largs shore, dreaming of long voyages and wondering if he could get all the way to the far shore and back before his number was called by the boat-hirer.

What he does instead is use the wee boat in order to look at other boats, row close to yachts or launches moored offshore and stare at them in love and longing, and envy the rich pigs who have such treasures, who actually *own* a boat, who never have to keep an eye on the pier clock to see if their hour is ending. The world is cruelly divided into people who have boats, and people who wish they had boats.

Boat people in Scotland are exactly the same as boat people everywhere; lunatics who will suffer any agony as long as it is suffered afloat. One freezing night I took a watch at the wheel of the old *Servabo*, a great lumpen ninety-foot converted Brixham trawler,

Clyde Week

steering by compass and faith down the Mull of Kintyre and mortal
cold to the marrow in six sweaters, and as I bleared at the compass
and heaved the rudder back and forth and shuddered, I wouldn't
have called the King my uncle. For misery like this, men will leave
wife and child and promotion.

Unfortunately, boats do breed a most un-Scottish snobbery. If
you are a panicky social climber, it's worrying not to be able to
classify other people by their accents, but you can classify them as
yachtsmen and non-yachtsmen, and you can subdivide the yachtsmen into admirable chaps with twelve-metres and uppity proles with
second-hand sailing dinghies. A funny thing happened to Allan Neill,
an Edinburgher who gave up acting to run a hotel in the fanatical
sailing village of Tighnabruaich. In time he acquired three specimens of the Loch Long, a twenty-one-foot keelboat with a big reputation in those waters and a beautiful thing to sail in, though they tell
me it will always turn downwind if you let the helm go. Nevertheless,
it is quite a lot of boat, and a big asset to a hotel where guests can sign
on for sailing courses as well as bed and board.

During a quiet spell, Neill had an itch to enter for some of the
races at Largs, and he set off with a friend as crew in one of the Loch
Longs. It sounds like a simple enough venture, sailing a good boat

for a few miles, but yachts don't run to schedule. You have to wait for wind and fight against it and do endless zigzags for miles to cover a few hundred yards. The Loch Long is a long thin boat consisting mostly of open cockpit, with a claustrophobic shelter at the front in which a man or two can crawl in and lie down in miserable discomfort and sleep if they have nowhere else to go.

By the time the boat got to Largs, the gallant sailors were a grubby pair in need of wash and shave, and Neill rowed ashore to have a quick drink before he could bear to look at himself.

Attempting to look invisible in a hotel bar, he became aware that he had suddenly been surrounded by high-class yachting people, men in faultless blazers and ornamental women with perfume and delicious coiffures, all together and under the command of a splendid citizen who was ordering drinks for everybody. He noticed the scruffy figure hiding at the end of the bar and called jovially,

'You'll have one too!'

(Poor sod, he's wandered into the wrong place, but we're all democratic here, the comradeship of the sea and everything.)

'It's all right,' Neill said humbly. 'I'm just having this one and going.'

(Cheeky slob, you know where you can put your drink.)

'Nonsense, man, have one, you look as if you need it.'

(One thing I will say, I've never been a snob.)

'Thank you very much, sir.'

(That 'sir' was a cunning move, he'll go for it like a drunk flounder.)

'What kind of dinghy are you sailing?'

'I'm on a Loch Long.'

'Oh? Oh. Who are you crewing for?'

'Actually, it's my own Loch Long.'

'Really!'

(Oh Lord, he must be a plumber's mate or a labourer, or something, one of those dogged types who spend all their wages buying a decent boat on the never-never to keep up with the Joneses.)

'Hoping for a win, eh?' said the citizen, resentment creeping into his joviality.

'I don't know,' Neill said. 'This weather doesn't really suit the *Shalom*. I would have had a better chance if I had brought the *Medora*.'

(Go on, collapse of stout party, you jumped-up get.)

'Eh, eh, eh, hey? Don't tell me you've got, ha ha, *two* Loch Longs! Ha ha.'

'No. I've got three, in fact.'

(Exit stage left, don't snigger, look thoughtful and abstracted, don't look back, collapse of stout party. *Now* snigger.)

Real sailing men tend not to be snobbish, except in their skills. People who own boats and sail them hard are always trying to get friendly with everybody, in the hope of finding somebody who will crew for them, regardless of race, colour or creed; just as long as they can find somebody who will jump like a rabbit when screamed at, and never answer back. The helmsman of a twelve-foot dinghy is just as much a Bligh as the skipper of an ocean-racing monster.

After hating them all for years, I gritted my teeth and got into the club by nailing together a tiny boat with a blunt end at both ends, and one tiny sail. I will say this for the hardened veterans, they laughed like hell. But there is nothing to compare with being handy to the Firth of Clyde and possessing an entire boat, even a tarred apple-box.

It is noticeable that the writings of sailing fiends fall into a pattern of yoicks-prang-play-it-cool prose and are concerned entirely with disasters, so let's get this over with. I took the boat out for the first time off the Arran shore, sailed in terror for fifteen minutes, and then turned inshore and smashed the rudder on a submerged rock. I took down the sail next day and tried it with a second-hand outboard engine which took half-an-hour to start and ran for two minutes, during which the boat never moved forward but simply whirled like a top. A year later I had repaired the rudder and found that by some magic, the boat had become functioning, and skimmed up and down the Kyles of Bute like a bird. Two days later, carelessly dumped on the beach below high-water mark, it vanished overnight.

High-water mark is a pretty important thing in the Firth of Clyde. Dinghy sailors who have become expert on reservoirs have been known to row ashore from their first salt-water cruise, tie up their dinghy and find it three hours later hanging in midair from a pier. But a missing yacht, even a tiny dinghy, is taken seriously on the Clyde. The distant police were informed, notes were taken, and the following day the missing vessel was reported aground on the Isle of Bute. The fey touch about this story is that it was found by a shepherd who was out looking for stray sheep. Amphibian sheep?

But within an hour of the news, six people who had no connec-

Near Gourock : fishermen

tion with the dinghy or its owner had found a motor launch and were away on a rescue mission that took all day. Sailing people love small disasters because it brings everybody together.

The Firth of Clyde is dramatic by nature. There's a night-club on the Island of Cumbrae, but the everlasting hills are oblivious. It was on Cumbrae that a minister once invoked the blessing of God on 'Cumbrae, and the adjacent islands of Great Britain and Ireland.'

Arran is the island of magic, which nobody has ever explained. It's only an island, after all, rather short of good pubs and other things. And it rains on Arran. It is possible to sit in glaring sunshine on the mainland sometimes and watch the island sitting grandiosely under an immovable umbrella of black cloud. But tourists who spend a month on the island come home brown and swashbuckling regardless. Maybe it's the peaty water.

Almost immune to the slick tricks of the tourist industry, the island drags people back year after year to what is almost a secret society. Among the natives, a feverish spiritual life rages. At any one moment you can find twenty-five drama groups operating on the island, and the next moment it may be twenty-six owing to the fissiparous nature of the Arran culture-lover. The place tends to crawl with artists in water-colours and oils and words and none of them

The Cloch lighthouse, Gourock

has any respect for the mainland at all. There was a tolerable murder on the island half-a-century ago, when a fool railwayman called Laurie climbed Goat Fell with Rose, an English tourist; pushed him off the top and robbed him of everything including a gold watch; and then walked jauntily down to the village of Corrie and tried to date up the barmaid in the local hotel while he was drinking his victim's money. The island also has the King's Cave, where Robert Bruce spent his exile and was tutored in courage by an anonymous spider. There are Bruce's Caves everywhere, it must be added. They were the staple industry of the islands in the fourteenth century.

Cynics have also suggested that Arran is a delusion, an artificial island skilfully erected from Airfix kits when the first tourist boat of the season is sighted. It could be, at that. I am always surprised to find it still there.

It is there nevertheless. The Clyde is after all real and not a dream. But if I were dreaming it up, I would dream it up just as it is.

CITY OF DREAMERS

So there I was, this windy afternoon, wearing a fibreglass helmet and carrying a tripod and looking like a right gomeril, walking across the River Tay from South to North on a row of slimy planks underneath the railway bridge and trying not to look at the water a mile below, and I was thinking to myself that if you have to go to Dundee, this is as good a way as any; because by the time you get there you'll be so happy to be *anywhere* that you'll love the place even if it's infested with insane tigers.

This entire proceeding was very Scotch, in that it demonstrated the equality of man. There was a wee crowd of us making a documentary film about gas-pipes, and there's a gas-pipe running along the Tay Bridge, so somebody had to take pictures of it. What puzzled me, every time my foot slipped and I grabbed at the hand-rail, was what I was supposed to be doing there gibbering with fear, because I was only the script-writer. In the movie business, as everybody knows, the script-writer is kept in a silken padded room and fed cooling drinks by long-legged starlets while the lower orders scramble over mountains and fall off buildings with their cameras and exposure meters.

In Scotland, the script-writer totes a tripod and slithers under bridges because there aren't enough lower orders to go round. The man in front of me was the Producer, in fact, and the reason why he was in front of me was that somebody had to carry the camera, and I thought it would be useful, if one of the planks was ready to break, to have him on it at the time and me well back and learning from his mistake. The one flaw in this scheme was that there is a wooden

Work in Progress:
The new Tay Bridge, Dundee

handrail on only one side of the cat-walk, and as he edged his way along, he gripped it so hard that bits of it were crushed to sawdust by the time I came along. If you really want to have adrenalin squirting out of your ears, you don't have to go to Africa and try out a pygmy rope bridge. You can die of fright at a tenth of the price above the Silvery Tay.

On such trips, the explorer can divert his mind from present horror by fixing his eyes on the ruined piers of the *other* Tay Bridge, and recollect that on a dark stormy night just before Hogmanay in 1879, the old bridge fell to bits with a trainload of railway customers. The first Tay Bridge was the pride of the starry-eyed age of Victorian know-how, and a thrilling epic poem was written to celebrate its splendour. There wasn't an East Coast Scotsman who didn't walk several inches taller in the knowledge that good Scotch engineering could lick anything, and it was pretty rotten for everybody when the wind blew the bridge away.

The main reason for this unhappy incident was that when the girders were hauled into place, half of the bolts wouldn't go through, and rather than waste time and disappoint the public, the engineer in charge devised a new gadget called Beaumont's Egg, a mixture of axle-grease and blacklead and metal filings, which could be rammed into the holes and stiffened with shellac and looked twice as good as iron. The invention has never caught on, however.

The Tay is nevertheless most beautiful to behold, even from underneath a bridge with the wind snarling through your socks. Any man of sensibility will agree with the words of William McGonagall, who addressed it thus:

Beautiful Silvery Tay,
With your landscapes, so lovely and gay
Along each side of your waters, to Perth all the way;
No other river in the world has got scenery more fine,
Only I am told the beautiful Rhine,
Near to Wormit Bay, it seems very fine,
Where the Railway Bridge is towering above its waters sublime
And the beautiful ship Mars,
With her juvenile Tars,
Both lively and gay,
Does carelessly lie
By night and by day,
On the beautiful Bay
Of the silvery Tay.
Beautiful, beautiful! silvery Tay,
Thy scenery is enchanting on a fine summer day,
Near by Balmerino it is beautiful to behold,
When the trees are in full bloom and the cornfields seems like
    gold –
And nature's face seems gay
And the lambkins they do play,
And the humming bee is on the wing,
It is enough to make one sing,
While they carelessly do stray,
Along the beautiful banks of the silvery Tay,
Beautiful silvery Tay, rolling smoothly on your way,
Near by Newport, as clear as the day,
Thy scenery around is charming I'll be bound . . .
And would make the heart of any one feel light and gay on a
    fine summer day
To view the beautiful scenery along the banks of the Silvery
    Tay.

Dundee was built on jute, and has a curious history of depopulation and repopulation to match the rise and fall of trade. The most
startling thing about the city, if you have come from the west, is that
it has the feel of a foreign country. The tenements and the narrow
streets and the opulent mansions built in rows by the jute barons are
no different from those in any other Scottish city, but the flavour of
the place is oddly sharp and remote, and more alien to a Glaswegian

than he would find New York or Pittsburg. I'm not complaining
about this; I always had a fine time in Dundee and the splendid Dundee Repertory Theatre had the reckless courage to produce my first
play. Soon afterwards it burned to the ground, which ought to be a
lesson to it. Aside from the theatre, which has dangerous cosmopo-
litan tendencies, the quality of the city is probably a firm concentra-
tion on its own affairs and to hell with lesser breeds. But Dundee,
wrapped up in its wee jute shell, has made an industry of creating
dreams for the whole British nation. This town gave birth to Chung
and Clicky-ba, to the Black Sapper and Captain Q, the Big Stiff and
Red Rock Baxter, Bingo the Black Streak and even Korky the Kat.
And the Broons.

Sturdy British boyhood has been enslaved for generations by the
arch-heroes of our time, punching and drilling and shooting their
way through the pages of *The Rover* and *The Adventure* and *The
Wizard* and *The Hotspur*. They were always published from an imposing address at Fetter Lane in London's newspaper belt, but that
was strictly a disguise. The whole shebang originates at the head
office in Dundee, where the D. C. Thomson press has a monopoly of
the dream traffic.

The father of this enterprise, the great D. C. Thomson, was a
press mogul with no resemblance to any of those flamboyant bodgers
who produce a couple of papers and then queue up for a peerage.
Not even a teeny-weeny knighthood for old Thomson. He was in
business, and business up the East Coast is a private, dignified affair
of making dough and keeping quiet about it. In addition to the boys'
papers, the Thomson Press always had a strong line in the kind of
weeklies that servant-girls were supposed to read, with bold names
like *The Oracle* and *The Red Star Weekly* and a strong Gothic strain
of entertainment. I used to be a hog for these when my sisters bought
them, and the stories that fed my appetites best were laced with
gypsy's warnings and dread premonitions, decorated with strap-lines
like *Her Wedding-Dress became Her Shroud*. I thought shrouds were
dandy, and so did the customers. While effete city-slicker publishers
in the south hire depth-motivation sharks to keep abreast of the
public taste, the Thomson outfit goes right ahead using its own uncanny judgment and turning out mountains of newsprint with its
own peculiar character, and selling all of them.

Thomson had the reputation of never trying anything that wasn't
a commercial success. The oatmeal folksiness of *The Sunday Post* is

Dundee: West Dock Street

an affront to zippy modern trends in journalism, but the paper goes right on selling to everybody in Scotland, and its corny old kitchen-comedy comic-strips The Broons and Oor Wullie are religiously posted to exiled relatives every week to keep their Scottishness fresh and pure. And the Thomson papers don't go in for the modern non-sense of big star personality writers with by-lines bigger than their stories. Practically the entire acreage of Thomson material appears anonymously, the product of a printing factory rather than of fallible human beings. In the newspaper business, in fact, the very word Dundee carries a superstitious awe and evokes an image of the great pulp-mill where writers and cartoonists clock on and take their places on a production line to fill their norm before the leg-irons are knocked off and they are released for the night. In my Glasgow boy-hood I used to be taken by a know-all friend past a house which was occupied, he told me, by the brother of *the Editor of The Wizard*! I didn't believe him. Editor of *The Wizard* indeed. Nobody edited *The Wizard*. It *happened*.

That was the Thomson magic at work. Every Thomson paper was an institution, a natural phenomenon, and if it had an editor, he certainly couldn't be the ordinary kind of man who would have brothers who could actually be seen cutting hedges or going for groceries. He would be . . . an *editor* . . . a *kind* of human being, but not the kind you meet. He was like God, all-knowing and all-loving, but unreachable except by prayer. The prayer took the form of the competitions for which you could win a football, or the joke-and-limerick page, where humble readers could try submitting some gag they had pinched from another Thomson paper and with luck, see their names in veritable print and receive half-a-dollar.

These occasional triumphs, these evidences that the Great Spirit was kindly, also revealed the vast influence of the Thomson boys' papers, because you only had to have your name published to receive a string of letters from what was then the Gold Coast.

'Dear sir, please send me a football and in return I will send you gold-dust, a monkey skin and the skull of a M'bongo M'bongo warrior.' Those Gold Coast chummies were right on the ball, but more important, they all read *The Rover*. I wonder if Nkrumah has managed to suppress *that*.

One of the innumerable Thomson legends declares that Winston Churchill approached the old boy to discuss how D.C. would rally his papers round Churchill when he was contesting a Parliamentary seat in Dundee. Thomson was so outraged by this insolence from a mere politician that he forbade the name of Winston Churchill to appear in any Thomson publication. Decades later, when Churchill was wartime Prime Minister and a hero to every patriotic publisher including Thomson, the writ still ran, and the great man was referred to in print as The Prime Minister; never by name.

The descendants of the great D.C. still run the pulp empire in the great family tradition. They live, one surmises, in tolerable comfort, in decent houses around Dundee, and some members of the dynasty may be seen early each morning arriving like any douce citizens by the ferry across the Tay and taking a bus to the office. In the middle of the day they are liable to turn up at Keiller's tearoom and go for the three-and-sixpenny businessman's lunch. None of your decadent London-type orgies of expense-account booze-ups for these staunch Dundonian millionaires. They are a model to us all.

Maybe there's something in the air up there that nourishes stern individualism. An entire book has been devoted to the Dundee worthies of the past, and they go in for bold positive names like Blue Jock and Tarry Dan, Belly Go First, Scabbie Joe, Honey Tam, Bung the Barrels, the Iron Horse, Snuffy Daw, Teapot Tam, Indigo Blue, and Leebie Threedie. And the greatest of these is Sir William Topaz McGonagall, poet and tragedian, Knight of the White Elephant, Burmah.

McGonagall is the greatest bad poet in English literature, and a man of such magnificence of character and dedication that the mind reels in contemplating him. He was of Irish extraction, like so many weird Scots, and was born in Edinburgh, but brought to Dundee in his youth and trained as a handloom weaver. It was impossible to make a living with the handloom, but as he has himself written, 'Dame Fortune has been very kind to me by endowing me with the genius of poetry. It was in the year of 1877, and in the month of June, when trees and flowers were in full bloom. Well, it being the holiday week in Dundee, I was sitting in my back room in Paton's Lane, Dundee, lamenting to myself because I couldn't get to the Highlands on holiday to see the beautiful scenery, when all of a sudden my body got inflamed, and instantly I was seized with a strong desire to write poetry, so strong, in fact, that in imagination I thought I heard a voice crying in my ears –

"WRITE! WRITE!"

I wondered what could be the matter with me, and I began to walk

A back kitchen,
near Broughty Ferry, Dundee

backwards and forwards in a great fit of excitement, saying to myself
– " I know nothing about poetry ". But still the voice kept ringing in
my ears until at last, being overcome with a desire to write poetry,
I found paper, pen, and ink, and in a state of frenzy, sat me down to
think what would be my first subject for a poem.'

McGonagall, in his frenzy, composed a quatrain in honour of a
Dundee minister, and it was instantly published in *The Weekly News*.
His next, or second poem, was the 'Railway Bridge of the Silvery

Tay,' which caused a great sensation in Dundee and far away. In fact, he wrote later, 'it was the only poem that made me famous universally. The reading of the poem abroad caused the Emperor of Brazil to leave his home far away incognito and view the bridge as he passed along en route to Inverness.'

Similar enthusiasm was constantly welling up in the breasts of exotic notables for the poetry of McGonagall. His title, Knight of the White Elephant, Burmah, was communicated to the bard in a letter from the Court of King Theebaw, Andaman Islands, dated December 2, 1894, and signed by C. Macdonald, K.O.W.E.B., the Poet Laureate of Burmah. According to Mr Macdonald, the Burmese king had lately been in a state of gloom, but on hearing some of McGonagall's works, had brightened up at once and become transformed. The letter in which this touching scene was described was enormous in size, and promised McGonagall that a real live white elephant, to go with the knighthood, was being sent to him at once. McGonagall was compelled to write declining the animal because his wife refused to have it in the house.

It's the easiest thing in the world to dismiss McGonagall as a harmless idiot, and many people do. But he was a legitimate eccentric, and his spirit was splendid and indestructible as well as ridiculous. He endured every horror and humiliation without ever despairing of his genius. His first appearance on the stage was in Mr Giles' Penny Theatre in Dundee, where he played Macbeth to unbounded applause. The crowd were so wild for McGonagall that the actors of the company, he realised, were very jealous, and several were so bold as to say so. 'And when it came to the combat scene betwixt me and Macduff, the actor who was playing Macduff tried to spoil me by telling me to cut it short, so as the audience, in his opinion, would say it was a poor combat, but I was too cute for him, guessing his motive for it. I continued the combat until he was fairly exhausted, and until there was one old gentleman in the audience cried out, "Well done, McGonagall! Walk into him!" And so I did until he was in a great rage, and stamped his foot, and cried out, "Fool! Why don't you fall?" And when I did fall the cry was "McGonagall! McGonagall! Bring him out! Bring him out!" until I had to come before the curtain and receive an ovation from the audience.'

Another of his strange adventures was his journey to Balmoral, to see the bonnie Highland flora and her Gracious Majesty the

on the waterfront, Dundee

Queen, who was living in Balmoral Castle. He walked all the way
from Dundee, was alternately sunburned and soaked, and on the
third day knocked at the lodge-gate. A surly menial tried to make a
fool of him and turned him away after the poet had refused to per-
form a selection of his works in the open air.

He took ship for America to seek the big dough, gave a wildly

Sammy Reid, and
the High St., Dundee

successful concert on board and was swindled out of the collection
money by a steward. New York was deaf to his talent and a kindly
hotel-keeper in Dundee sent him the money for his fare home. Next
he left to seek his fortune in London, largely because he had acquired the odd notion that Dion Boucicault was a fan and anxious to
meet him. Boucicault never saw him, London spurned him, and the
dauntless bard returned to Scotland. Humorous chaps were always
organising McGonagall recitals at which long clumsy practical jokes
were to be played on the genius, but he suffered them all with pity
rather than rancour, and kept bashing away at the deathless verse.

'I am a playwright as well as a poet. My magnum opus in this
direction is a manuscript which took me six months to compose,
and nearly half that time to write out. It is a tragedy of the Shake-
spearean type, and is entitled Jack o' the Cudgel, in seven acts. I tried
to keep it in the legitimate bounds of five acts, but became so intensely absorbed in my subject that the end of act five was reached
with barely half of my characters killed. In this dilemma what was I
to do? Two modes of procedure presented themselves. I could re-
write it, in a condensed form, which would enable me to dispose of
my heroes and heroines with less talk and more action; or I could let
the plot run to its natural conclusion irrespective of its length, and
allow the party to whom I sold it to cut it down to suit himself, or
make two plays of it for that part, so long as I got my money for it.
This course I eventually decided to adopt, entirely for the reason
that, so well pleased was I with its contents and general arrangement,
that I could not bring myself to alter a single syllable. It is simply
perfect in phraseology, balance, design, plot and general excellence,
so I finished it, and carefully put it past as a source of income if I
happened to fall on evil times.'

An actor of the day offered McGonagall half-a-crown, and the
outraged author wrenched the precious manuscript back and
shouted, 'Sir, if that tragedy was boiled in muck you would not get a
spoonful of the broth for half-a-crown.'

McGonagall was in the right. The celebrated actor, Gardner
Coyne, has vanished without trace, but the poet's name lives on. He
took Glasgow by storm, and although his concert there was adorned
with the routine gimmicks of letters of apology from foreign ambas-
sadors, and presided over by a German Baron, and although the poet
was induced, in the jollity of the atmosphere, to take off most of his
clothes and hand them round for admirers to touch, nobody actually

threw anything at him, and the audience collected £4 15s. to pay McGonagall for their fun. It was this lavish generosity that inspired one of his finest works; which contains the following lines:

> O, beautiful city of Glasgow which stands on the river Clyde,
> How happy should the people be which in ye reside,
> Because it is the most enterprising city of the present day,
> Whatever anybody else may say.
> O, wonderful city of Glasgow, with your triple expansion
>   engines
> At the making of which your workmen get many singeins;
> Also the deepening of the Clyde, most marvellous to behold,
> Which cost much money, be it told.
> Then there is a grand picture gallery
> Which the keepers thereof are paid a very large salary;
> Therefore, citizens of Glasgow, do not fret or worry,
> For there is nothing like it in all Edinburgh.
> And the happiest night I ever spent
> Was in Glasgow, where I got as much as pay my rent
> From your merchant princes most fine
> Who likewise sang a song to me called Clementine;
> Which was most beautiful to hear, also a dance
> Round and round, all singing at once;
> And the treatment I got in Glasgow, I must confess,
> Was even better than Inverness.
> Oh, beautiful city of Glasgow, I must conclude my lay,
> By calling thee the greatest city of the present day;
> For your treatment of me was by no means churlish,
> Therefore I say, 'Let Glasgow flourish.'

In a footnote, the poet added that 'In this beautiful and exhaustive, descriptive poem, I have omitted all reference to the stripping episode, because the poem, which is built to last longer than the prose on which it is set, will be read centuries after the autobiography has been consigned to forgetfulness.'

And after all, he was right. McGonagall is not merely a Victorian versifier, he is now an art form, and dozens of literate blokes in modern times have used the McGonagall formula. The greatest of these was probably the late Donald McNaughton, a magnificently histrionic Glaswegian who had all the presence of a great actor-

manager and was one of the greatest pub conversationalists in history. Donald was working for *The Sunday Mail* in Glasgow when the paper was bought over by the mammoth Mirror Group, and when the new masters were touring the building, they came upon him sitting quietly at his desk staring into the distance with a look of burning intelligence.

'What's your job!' one of them asked, quite amiably. McNaughton looked up calmly and said, 'Poet and Tragedian.' McGonagall would have been proud of him.

THE SIGHT

Just as every shanty Irishman is descended from the Kings of Ireland, every Scotsman fancies that he probably has second-sight, if
only he could lay his hands on it. Every now and then I get blurred
intimations of my own hidden powers, because of my over-active
dream life. One night I dreamed of a fire, and sure enough, there
was a fire somewhere in the South of England less than a month
later. Recently my performances have improved, though. I dream
about snails, and the very next day somebody mentions snails,
though snails have simply not occurred to anybody for months. Or I
dream about insurance, and the bill for the premium arrives promptly
on the following morning. The curse is, of course, that none of these
uncanny premonitions has any cash value. I keep trying to dream
about horse-races, but nothing happens at all. Or maybe the difficulty with second-sight is that you can't recognise a prediction until
after the thing has actually happened; which doesn't seem like an
efficient way to run a business.

There are all sorts of fey folk running about in Scotland, all the
same, and the wise plan is to run shrieking if you ever meet one.
Second-sight tends to concentrate on death and disaster for everybody in sight – including the prophet, sometimes.

The greatest of the legendary Scottish visionaries was Kenneth
Mackenzie, a frightening peasant born at the beginning of the
seventeenth century and nicknamed the Brahan Seer since he
worked near the Highland estate of Brahan. Mackenzie was at the
predicting business incessantly, if all the stories are to be believed,

and I for one don't believe half of them. When anybody lived as long ago as that, and became a legend, everybody who likes second-sight stories gets hypnotised by the delight of the thing and claims that every single thing that happens was mentioned *somewhere* by the old boy.

Still, the legends make nice copy, since there are so many of them. Mackenzie, it is alleged, predicted that carriages would run through the Highlands without horses and, of course, they did. He said that Drummossie's bleak moor would be stained with the best blood of the Highlands, and a century and a half later, the battle of Culloden was arranged. Some of his promises were regarded as ludicrous, of course, as when he said that a cow would give birth to a calf in the uppermost chamber of Fairburn Tower, a proud and private mansion. Nevertheless, the place fell into ruin, and when workmen were making restorations, a cow did walk up the now exposed staircase, lured by odd bits of hay that had been dropped, and obligingly delivered on the top storey. Aye, well, it's a good story.

The Seer's cryptic utterances didn't bother folk very much, however, since there wasn't much entertainment about in those days and a bit of mumbo-jumbo was better than nothing. But an ugly come-uppance was in store for him, and it's rather odd. It fell about that another Kenneth Mackenzie, the third Earl of Seaforth, was away from home and in Paris, on some affair of state, and his Countess began to worry about his long absence and the lack of news. The Seer was summoned and ordered to summon news from his private sources, and he thought hard and then tried to pass it off.

'Be satisfied,' he declared, 'that your lord is well and merry.'

The Countess didn't think this brief paragraph was worth the money, and insisted on more. Now this is where, it seems to me, the Seer's powers let him down badly. If he had known as much as a professional prophet should, he would have kept his mouth shut. But the Countess was a hard bitch, and maybe he was in only partial touch with the future. When she got stubborn, he finally revealed to her that the Earl was in good health, in fine clothes, sitting on a fine chair with a pretty woman on his knee. The Countess was absolutely livid, as people often are when they get what they asked for. Other people were listening, and a tale like this was an affront to a noble family. In a spitting rage, she ordered Mackenzie to be burned to death as a witch. Nobody has been able to find any record of this official incineration, but that doesn't necessarily mean it didn't happen. The Seer, according to tradition, thought she was kidding, but he didn't know Countesses as well as he knew the future, and he soon discovered that he was for the fire in earnest.

Thereupon he delivered his final prediction, and it was a beauty.

'The line of Seaforth will end in extinction and sorrow. The last of the house will be both deaf and dumb. He will be the father of four sons, all of whom he will follow to the tomb. He will live careworn and die mourning, knowing that the honours of the line are to be extinguished forever. His possessions will be inherited by a white-hooded lassie from the East, and she is to kill her sister.

'And as a sign that these things are coming to pass, there shall be four great lairds in the days of the last deaf and dumb Seaforth, of whom one will be buck-toothed, another hare-lipped, another half-witted, and the fourth a stammerer.'

Now this is the kind of prophecy you can respect. Nothing vague or Delphic, but the facts and plenty of them.

The last Earl was Francis Humberston Mackenzie, who was not deaf and dumb at all, but became deaf after an attack of scarlet fever. To make this more agreeably Gothic, the lad had a delirious dream as he lay ill, in a dormitory with several schoolmates who had also been stricken in the epidemic. In this dream he saw a lady going round the dormitory choosing certain boys and *hammering spikes into their skulls*. This nightmare, as reported when he wakened, was so specific that the doctor noted the names of the boys, and was startled to find later that those very boys, and no others, died of the fever.

The Earl, however, didn't let his deafness worry him too much. He was created a British peer in 1797, raised a regiment, became a famous soldier, married and had four sons. All of them died.

In Napoleonic times, as it happened, Seaforth's neighbours in Scotland included McKenzie of Garloch, Chisholm of Chisholm, Grant Baronet of Grant, and Macleod of Raasay. They suffered respectively from buck teeth, hare-lip, dim wits and a stammer. The Earl died on January 11, 1815.

His possessions descended to his eldest daughter Mary, who had married Admiral Sir Samuel Hood and was living with her husband in the Far East. Note the concatenation of detail, even to the name Hood. But more than that, her husband died soon afterwards, and she returned home wearing a *widow's hood*. She re-married, and everything was dandy, but one day there was a lamentable occurence when she was out driving with her sister Caroline in a pony-cart. The pony bolted and both women were thrown from the cart. Caroline died of her injuries.

Do not, therefore, listen to Highland seers; or, if you can't avoid listening, refrain from burning them afterwards.

INTO THE UNKNOWN

There are some places whose very names reek of romance, but which remain unvisited and mysterious even though they're only an hour away. It's easy enough to get to Paris or Rome, but Twechar, for instance, remains a tantalising name on a map; and Tomintoul, and Saltburn, and Muir of Ord. They sing strangely on the tongue, and there are only two things you can do if you want to exorcise them: get up and go, or leave them lying on the map and persuade yourself that you must never see them or some hideous destiny will catch up with you. If you spend years wondering about some silly place-name, the chances are that it's trying to drag you towards it to finish you off.

Bo'ness was always one of those places. Bo'ness. Bo'ness. If you whisper it over and over, it turns into the shrill, menacing cry of a ghostly railway porter swirling along a midnight wind. But it became irresistible.

I went with my brother-in-law, because nobody likes to face the unknown alone. We both wore beards, as talismans. Superficially, this started out as a merry jaunt in pursuit of the sporting life. Motoring clubs used to hold hill speed trials at Bo'ness, and we were absolutely hipped on motor sport at the time, in the obsessional degree found only among those who have never owned a car. We lusted for cars, and could conduct debates on the merits of hemispherical and wedge-shaped combustion chambers and de Dion axles and roll centres and slip angles and the lot. We exercised the true connoisseurship of pure theory and we secretly detested people who were so loutish as to own cars in the crude physical sense; but we were drawn helplessly towards them and we finally prepared an expedition one cold Saturday to see the accursed hill speed trials. We knew we would hate everybody there, but we could love the machines and remain mysterious and aloof from the swine who drove them.

We practised an aggressive form of poverty, which wasn't difficult, because there is something obscene about travelling to a motor sport event on a bus, and we carried bundles of cheap, nasty sandwiches with an air of defiance which nobody noticed. We ate the lot ten minutes after we got on the bus because this is the Scots peasant tradition. Whenever he travels anywhere, the scruffy Scotsman totes a load of indigestible food under his arm, wrapped in brown paper, and he starts to wolf it as soon as he's moving, being convinced in his heart that he will never arrive so he might as well have the good of it at once.

It takes two buses to get from Glasgow to Bo'ness. The first arrives at Falkirk, which is perfectly okay as small industrial towns go, but it is never any surprise on arrival to find the local population queuing up for buses to get to hell out and into Glasgow for the unhealthy Saturday excitements of the big city.

We lined up at the other stance to catch a bus deeper into the hinterland and to Bo'ness, conscious that we were shaking civilisation from our feet. The city slicker on these little local bus routes has the positive feeling of alienation, as he would have in a bus in rural Mexico, because although the language is the same, the accent has unexpected intonations and elisions, and the conversations are private and mysterious, relating to strange, tiny, local events and characters. In this environment, clearly, such a thing as a hill speed trial would be a fleeting foreign intrusion, ignored by the populace. The strangers from the city would descend on the place and roar their silly engines and then vanish, and the stubborn peace of the countryside would close in again unshaken. Nobody on the bus could possibly be going to the trials. Nobody on the bus could be going anywhere identifiable, in fact. Passengers dropped off at whimsical spots in a deserted land and disappeared.

Pretty soon Fergus began to show signs of suppressed excitement, like an old dog smelling something familiar, because he had actually been to Bo'ness once before, and was sure he could even identify the field in which the silly trials were held. We started looking furtively for temporary road signs and posters, and saw none.

'Look,' Fergus suddenly muttered, 'that's the place they held it

Boness

last time, that field. It *looks* like it,' he added doubtfully. There was nothing in sight but two pigs.

From among the rhubarb of rustic chatter on the top deck of the bus, one voice suddenly emerged clearly.

'Eh, some motor races in there last week, Boab. See it? Quite a crowd, there wis.'

We looked thoughtful and suave and got off the bus in a hurry and walked back. The field was still there, with a lot of churn marks from tyres, and a bit of wet paper that might have been a poster a week before. This may sound like a routine piece of inefficiency, but you can believe me that there is something particularly stricken about standing on the outskirts of Bo'ness on a dull Saturday afternoon with nothing to do but look at an empty field. We stared at the mud and tried to force crowds of jolly laughing speed trialists to appear, but nothing happened. We didn't look at each other. We waited for the bus coming back to Falkirk, and when it came it was crammed with passengers and roared past. The only thing left to do was to walk right into Bo'ness and catch the next bus.

It was a walk through a slit in the time-space continuum. No human person appeared, and as we came closer to the village we felt like figures against an old etching. A factory rose on the right of the road and we stared at it without believing it. The brick exterior was black with time and the windows were buried in grime, but most disquieting were the proportions of the thing.

It had an indeterminate number of storeys, but each appeared to be only five or six feet high, and the little windows were squashed down into caricatures of windows. It was the original black satanic mill, and the sight of it chilled the blood. We realised it must have been built by a craggy Victorian industrialist who knew he could fill it with tiny, misshapen serfs capable of living out their brief pallid lives with the ceilings squashing down on them, and a malignant dwarf foreman scuttling along between the workbenches with a rope's-end.

'Come to bonnie Scotland,' Fergus said nervously.

'The land of hills and heather,' I said, but I had started to walk faster, because ahead in the distance there appeared the gable-end of a stone cottage bearing the bold painted legend, 'Wines and Spirits,' and it came to me that in the remote outback a lot of pubs are open till three in the afternoon. Fergus had instantaneously thought alike, and we broke into a shambling run, it now being five minutes to three. We were still shambling when we heard a heavy door slam shut. Bo'ness had defeated us.

But what had happened to the people? As we shuffled into a village square thing, we saw rows of shops firmly closed and deserted. A tiny cinema was adorned with a doorman, but by this time we knew he would turn out to be a pasteboard cut-out. Bo'ness had become a ghost town as soon as we decided to visit it.

Then we saw the people. They were lined right round the far end of the square, and what they were doing was waiting to catch the next bus into Falkirk. If you live in Bo'ness, Falkirk on a Saturday afternoon represents the champagne thrill of Montmartre. I never have seen a hill speed trial, anywhere. I found I had outgrown the idea.

Haddington is a different proposition altogether. The Lothians are among the blessed corners of Scotland, with a rich feminine landscape of swelling curves and the fresh sweet smell of money. Nature had been kind to this land, and man has not raped it. The villages are solidly graceful and the air is sweet and you could write a song about it in a minute. All the same, it keeps the faint intriguing flavour of strangeness to an incomer, because quite a lot of people *shoot* things down there, and I can never think of anything odder than that. It was a few miles from Haddington that I turned up one afternoon to meet a man who had some kind of story to tell, and I had to meet him there because he was a busy character and he was engaged that day in a big carry-on involving some new breed of gun-dog, a Swiss combination lurcher-pointer-setter or something of the kind, which I was assured was going to be the coming thing in high-class pot-lickers.

I took my wife and two dear toddlers that time, and the kids were all for it, because we had suddenly got rich and had a wee spartan motor car only four years old, in which everything *worked*.

My wife wasn't entirely enthusiastic.

'I don't want to see anything getting shot,' she protested.

'Neither do I,' I said. I wasn't sure whether I wanted to see anything get shot or not. 'They usually miss,' I said insincerely. I disapproved of things getting shot, but I knew in myself the suppressed traces of primitive viciousness and the excitement of murder. It's because I have sadistic impulses that I hate violence.

'It's like a bullfight,' I said. 'It's rotten and nasty, but if you were in Madrid you wouldn't want to miss the spectacle, just once.'

'We're not in Madrid,' she said reasonably, but she was spreading meat paste and bananas on brown bread. The children were mad for meat paste and bananas that year. So was I, if it comes to that.

This time we arrived on the right Saturday, but we realised right away that we had arrived among a race that had never heard of meat paste and bananas. The assembled company was dragging tuck-baskets out of Bentley boots and tearing up whole turkeys to hand round. The man I had come to see offered me a couple of pounds of cold turkey, but my dignity was stronger than greed. I lay on the floor of the car and secretly ate a banana. It was miserably cold that day. After the orgy, the cars formed in a crocodile and zoomed off to a field where the big event was to occur.

The place had all the convenience of an arena. The field lay in a hollow, thirty feet below the level of the road, and it was planted thickly with kail nearly ready for harvesting. Among this vegetation, I learned, the hired hands had spent some hours planting live pheasants. This news impressed me deeply. In my proley ignorance, I had always thought of county people going through the horrors of hell stumbling across quagmires to get a shot at a flight of wild sullen

Lisa : a student, Dundee

game. It had never struck me that the thing could be arranged like an industrial operation, or that pheasants *liked* getting shot at.

The man I had come to see gave me a quick explanation of the game, which was to test the individual dogs for their skill and inbred cunning. The animals would be released a few at a time, and with masterly precision they would quarter the area, scientifically covering every foot of ground and scaring the pheasants into the air. Thereupon their owners would shoot the pheasants.

'That's not sport, it's an open-air abattoir,' Anna said, and I reckoned she was right. I felt it would have been more interesting if somebody developed a breed of pheasant that could shoot back. But everything is valuable experience, so we stood and shivered in the wind and stared down at the field of kail.

The first magnificent dogs were released, and to our delight, they went through that kail like lunatics, yelling their heads off and falling over one another in all directions at once. Pretty soon there was an impenetrable carpet of pheasants hovering about nine feet from the ground, and the sportsmen, bred to the trigger, were banging away from directly underneath it. They didn't hit a flaming thing.

So I still believe that all experience is valuable. And if I live long enough in Scotland, I'll get it.